Wisdom Keepers

Insightful Guidance From
Today's Sages

Compiled by
Kyra Schaefer

Wisdom Keepers

Copyright © 2022. All rights reserved. The author is responsible for their individual opinions expressed through their words. The author retains the copyright to this book. No part of this publication may be reproduced, distributed, or transmitted to any form or by any means, including photocopying, recording, or other electronic mechanical methods, without the prior written permission of the publisher.

As You Wish Publishing, LLC
Connect@asyouwishpublishing.com

ISBN-13: 978-1-951131-44-9

Library of Congress Control Number: 2022903421

Printed in the United States of America.

Nothing in this book or any affiliations with this book is a substitute for medical or psychological help. If you are needing help please seek it.

Table of Contents

Life Isn't Always Fair
By Holly Bird 1

Traditions
By Rose Bourassa 11

The Wisdom Within
By AJ Cavanagh 25

'Tis The Season: A Holy Day Rant
By Anne Foster Angelou 39

Learning to Quit
By Karen Gabler 51

This Little Light of Mine
By Sarah Gabler 65

Reflections for Everyday Life
By Jaime Lee Garcia 77

Our Memories Sustain Us
By Patricia Holgate Haney 93

Almost Home
By Marianne Hudspeth 109

Flying Through Fear: How to Change Everything
By Donna Kiel 123

When Opportunity Knocks, Open The Door
By Amy I. King 137

Being Beautifully Boxed
By Paula Meyer 149

Stepping Into the Crone Wisdom
By Maggie Morris 159

Ancora Imparo – Yet, I Am Learning
By Melissa Nelson Curran 173

Our Childhood Memories and Their Wisdom: My Kindergarten Tour
By Pedram Owtad 187

Becoming Wise Through My Eyes
By Talia Renzo 199

The Treasure You Call by Your Name
By Michelle Ann Ryan 213

Chapter

Life Isn't Always Fair
By Holly Bird

Holly Bird

Holly Bird, MS., is the international, best-selling author of, *Shaken Dreams, A Journey from Wife to Caregiver*, co-author of *When Angels Speak, 52 Weeks of Gratitude Journal, Kindness Crusader*, and *Ordinary Oneness*. Holly is a mentor and certified aging life coach, with a focus on aging, health, education, and family. She shares her wealth of life experiences—everything from spiritual and family mentoring, to marriage, gardening, cooking, traveling, and her favorite, being a grandma—on her blog.

Connect with Holly:

http://www.Hollysbirdnest.com

HollyBird@hollysbirdnest.com

Facebook @hollysbirdnest

Facebook @loveyourangels

Twitter @HOLLYJBIRD

Life Isn't Always Fair

By Holly Bird

As we take time to look around the world we live in today, there are thousands, if not millions, of people on social media and others writing books telling you to follow them and your life will magically change—that they hold the secret to life, and you will succeed as they have. As it seems today, everyone wants to be a "brand" and to become household names, but most are not showing the side of them that is *not* the brand. They are a made-up brand that others should be drawn to, leaving others in awe of their perfection, and even some that are in their early twenties, who have experienced very little life, trying to be life coaches and "coaching" everyone on how they should live their lives! No one is perfect, and no one has the answer, but when you are searching for a change in your life, it means you are ready to see your life differently, ready for a change, and again, I said, *your* life and *your* perspective on what and how you want your life to be.

Life isn't always easy or even fair. We look around, and there is so much turmoil that it can bring us all into a confused state of mind. But there is also so much good, and if we look hard enough, there is always something to be grateful for. When in doubt or fearful, it seems that we just need to take the next forward step, without looking behind us. But for some reason, our past seems to haunt us—swirling around in our heads like a tornado that has not

CHAPTER 1 | LIFE ISN'T ALWAYS FAIR

touched down but is leaving damage in its path and affecting our future forever—without us even knowing that our past is what has made us who we are and how we think. Letting go is not as easy as some would like us to believe, so, even a small step forward is better than staying in the past. To reach your goals, you must keep moving forward.

No matter how old you are, whether it be 23 or 103, you have a past and a future when waking every morning—even just the day before is your past—and learning to make peace with your past so it won't mess up the present is the only way that you can move on. You will never be able to remove some thoughts of your past, but you will be able to find ways to use them to see things with clarity and gratitude. You made it through those bad days, let's make today a better day!

So many people don't realize that only they can release and let go of the past and the fears that come from it. The best way, is to find something positive in every situation. In my own life, I have faced loss. I've had five miscarriages and experienced the live birth of a child who died hours later. This loss was in my early twenties, and the one thing I wanted more than anything was to be a mom. After I lost my son, Mathew, it was during the grieving process that I felt gratitude for the doctors, nurses, ambulance drivers, and helicopter pilots who tried so hard to save his life. That gratitude started to take over my heart, and I learned a small lesson that gratitude would help me get over a loss that I never thought I would.

A few months later, as I was spending time with my family, I woke up one morning and my mom said to me, "Good morning, beautiful!" I knew that I looked horrible—hair standing up on end, and I had a rough night with tears and frustration—but that statement made me feel so good, I could feel a smile and easiness taking over inside me. From that moment on, every time I wake up in the morning, I look at myself in the mirror and say, "Good morning, beautiful," and I can feel the smile that I felt the first time my mom said it to me.

I had learned this lesson of self-appreciation at a young age, but I also saw and felt so many other things that would frustrate and sometimes even aggravate me, that I started to use the "one statement trick" for many things in my life. Most of them kept me focused on the positive path that I knew I wanted to take in my life, but some ended up being life quotes that I would use all the time.

In my earlier adult years, my thoughts were to make money and never have to struggle like my parents did while I was growing up, but my mom had breast cancer, and there was a gnawing feeling inside of me that I needed to be there for her. No, it wasn't guilt, it was an awareness that many people learn much later in life, if at all—your job won't take care of you when you are sick; your friends and family will, so take care of them, it will be worth it!

As some of my friends were skyrocketing to success, I was taking care of family and struggling to finish school. I would sit in lectures, feeling like I already knew what the professor was going to say—that my life experiences had been the best education, and some of my failures had taught me that you don't have to win all the time, stay true to yourself, be kind, and admit when you're wrong. During

CHAPTER 1 | LIFE ISN'T ALWAYS FAIR

those lessons, I also found that crying *with* someone was more healing than crying alone.

Crying is a healthy way to relieve emotional stress and release hormones that help relieve both physical and emotional pain, so those old wives' tales about how "crying is for weak people" are wrong! It's also okay to let your children see you cry. And let them cry if they need to! Helping your children to maintain emotional balance in their lives will help them with success and in learning that failures can be disappointing. Allowing yourself a chance to heal from those will help them to look positively into their future, a lesson that can help us all to grow!

Sometimes crying can bring on what I call "emotional comparing" and the dreaded "what ifs." Don't compare your life to others; however good or bad your life is, it will change. Always be prepared and be ready to go with the flow, as you might be struggling one minute and the next, something amazing happens. It is never too late to be happy, but it is up to you. No one can give you the happiness you are looking for. Your happiness begins and ends with you, and no matter how significant someone is in your life, your happiness is not their responsibility. In today's world, we hear the saying "Happy wife, happy life," but the same thing goes for other individuals. They can't make you happy just by giving you your way, and that is a huge responsibility to put on your spouse. Needless to say again, but no one can make you happy—it is up to you to choose happiness!

Relationships can be difficult, especially if the world is seeing so many fake relationships on social media and television. If it has to be kept a secret, you should get out of it! Before you say, "I do," make sure that you *do* and that you are not trying to fix someone else to make yourself happy. Go into a marriage filled with self-love, so that you are putting yourself in the relationship to add to your love and to be willing to enhance your love and commitment to each other. Getting married is not about the wedding; it is about how a happy life makes for a content husband *and* wife! Remember, in your marriage, every day is special. Use the nice sheets, wear the fancy lingerie, burn candles, and wear your favorite cologne—you don't need an "occasion"!

What Happened?

There is so much that a life counselor or mentor wants to share. The list is long and it's also exciting when you know in your heart that if you can help even one person make a positive change in their life, the ripple effect can change the lives of so many. As I have a lot to write about, I was extremely excited to be included in this book of amazing Wisdom Keepers who are sharing to bring a positive flow of love and caring to the world. I love writing, but this contribution was one I procrastinated about because we were limited in the words we could share. I knew I was going to have life-changing cervical fusion surgery. I had lost the use of my arms and had numbness in my hands, making it difficult to write. I couldn't look down because of the five levels in my neck that are fused, and that was a complication that I never thought would happen. As I said above, I try very hard to not think about the "what ifs" but in this case, I should have.

CHAPTER 1 | LIFE ISN'T ALWAYS FAIR

I was excited to know that I was going to be able to type, write, and share. It had been months, but my complication, which at the time of this publication I can now share, was that a vertebra was broken in my neck, leaving me in worse pain, numbness—now in both arms—and total frustration. Why had I waited? Why was this happening? And of course, because of the lesson I am sharing with readers about life not being fair, I kept trying to find a new name, but between the pain medication and my internal dialog, I realized the title was perfect!

Some of the important lessons above are ones that are not talked about and that are always looked at differently, depending on the person who is sharing their wisdom and life stories, but they are the ones that will make a difference in your life today:

- Forgive yourself; it's the most important gift you can give yourself!
- Forgive others; you have no idea what their journey is all about.
- What other people think of you is none of your business. (Read that again!)
- Time heals almost everything if you allow it!
- Choose life, don't audit it. Show up and make the most of it now.
- Growing old beats the alternative of dying young.
- Take a deep breath, and count to ten. It calms the mind.

- Envy is a waste of time. Accept what you already have, not what you want

For those that believe in the grace and goodness of God, finding ways every day to be grateful will help you through the good times and bad.

- Believe in miracles; they are everywhere
- God loves you because of who God is, not because of anything you *did* or *didn't* do.
- Everything can change in the blink of an eye—but remember, God never blinks.
- Allow your character to be stronger and grateful in every circumstance.
- It's okay to get angry with God. He can take it. And he forgives us, just ask! He will never leave your side.

Life isn't tied with a bow, but it's still a gift, whether you have a spiritual connection that helps you through or you try to depend on yourself. There is always a way to find that life isn't always fair, but the choices you make are always your choice and the same for those around you. When we make choices, it can affect others, so they might feel their life is unfair too!

The one thing we all can do is to be our own best friend and love ourselves, and when we do, we will be loved! Life is too short – enjoy it!

Chapter Two

Traditions
By Rose Bourassa

Rose Bourassa

Rose Bourassa is a retired procurement specialist and international bestselling author. She is currently preparing for a second career as an evidential medium. She is a mother, grandmother, student, teacher, artist, and volunteer.

She strives to learn something new every day to keep sharp, and hopefully, something to help keep up with grandkids—even when they have to dumb it down! You can reach Rose via email at Remnick@aol.com

Traditions

By Rose Bourassa

Oh, how I loved the play, *Fiddler on the Roof*—the movie, the music, the story of life and traditions. I realized just how many traditions fall by the wayside from generation to generation. Once upon a time, our mothers taught us to sew, crochet, and cook from scratch. In many homes, a second language was taught.

Not in mine, though. Both of my grandparents on my mothers' side migrated here from Italy. My father's father came through Ellis Island from Greece. He was lucky enough to have his Greek name shortened to something more English-sounding. I do not recall much about my father's side of the family; they all called Chicago home, while California was our home. I know that Mom and Dad had met in Chicago and lived there until my father was discharged from the Army. That is when they all (and I do mean all—my mother's family included) moved to Southern California.

Growing up, we did not have much of a Greek influence in our lives—no second language, no Greek cooking. We did spend August in Chicago every year visiting the family. During the hottest time of year, we drove for a week to get there, stayed for three weeks, and then drove back in a week. I was not sure who my parents used as a travel agent, but I swore I would never use them! It was nice to have some Greek cooking for a while. I wish I had been old

CHAPTER 2 | TRADITIONS

enough during those trips to learn to cook some of the foods.

Watching the movie, *My Big Fat Greek Wedding*, made me realize how much I had missed out on growing up. But then, I think my dad was really more Italian than Greek.

Both my grandparents on Mom's side were fluent in Italian, as was my mother. Not us kids, though. None of us ever learned Italian. It was not because we didn't want to, just that Mom didn't feel the need for us to know it. Mom and Grandma used Italian as a secret code to talk with each other whenever there was business to discuss that we kids were not supposed to understand. Of course, we always knew when we were the subject of conversation! Sometimes I wish my mom had taught us Italian. You could tell from the tone of their voices that you were the topic of discussion. It would have been nice to know Italian as a second language. It would have come in so handy during the two years I lived with my grandmother. Our conversations would start in English, and midway through, she would turn to Italian, and I had to figure out what she was saying. Luckily, I had three years of Spanish in school, and the two are similar, both romance languages. By the end of the two years, I understood Italian. It was difficult for me to respond, but we managed to understand each other.

My mother was an excellent seamstress. She could make anything. She made my wedding dress from ideas I pulled from several different dresses. It was very easy for her. I could not sew a 5/8-inch straight seam to save my life. While in sewing class in middle school, I learned the teacher disagreed with my mother on sewing practices. My teacher was unaware that my mother had been a professional seamstress and worked for some big names before us kids came along. Mom had been sewing since she was three. She learned from her mom. If you did not follow Mom's instructions on cutting a pattern and how to put it together and which thread to use, you may as well not do it. I promptly took apart that first completed school project I brought home and resewed it following my mother's instructions. When I wore it to school the following week, my sewing teacher was upset that I had ruined the garment by redoing it. What was I thinking? Caught between the two, I dropped the class and did not sew again until my daughter was in her high school sewing class. Mom was way older, her sight was failing, but she could feel that seam and knew it was not 5/8-inch or straight! All those years wasted—I should have been learning at the feet of the master. Had I tried harder to master sewing, I still would not have been able to hem a pair of pants evenly.

When I was growing up, my grandmother baked her bread from scratch. She tried to teach me how to do it once, but she decided I did not have the wrist strength for kneading the dough—end of the lesson. I can make bread from scratch in a couple of different ways, none of which remotely resemble my grandmother's. I did, however, excel at baking Easter bread. This bread is made by weaving the dough into a basket and placing a raw decorated egg in the middle. After the bread has been baked, the egg is hard. It's delicious and pretty to look at. I do not make it every year, but I should. When I do make it, I cheat. I use my stand mixer for kneading the dough—my way to get around not

CHAPTER 2 | TRADITIONS

having the wrists to accomplish the task. Grandma's recipe for Easter bread works well in my mixer. My daughter loves to eat Easter bread. My granddaughter loves to make the braids. Hopefully, one of them will carry on this tradition.

Grandma's sister, my great aunt Mary, was another excellent cook. She would go into the kitchen and throw stuff into a bowl, and something extraordinary always resulted. Me, I had to measure. I always followed the recipe. She hated it when I put everything into a measuring cup before throwing it in the mixing bowl. I still measure everything. I follow recipes carefully, except when it comes to the family recipe for biscotti. That is where I will use my palm to measure out the anise seeds. Do I know how much to use via a measuring spoon? Of course, I do, but this is the only ingredient for which I will use my great aunt's teaching method. You can never have too much anise seed in biscotti! And a palm-full is always the right amount. Once upon a time, both my grandmother and my great aunt learned to cook before recipes existed. Both women had that knack of being able to open up the cupboard doors and whip up a family meal from nothing.

One of the best things my grandmother made was homemade pasta. She would mix the flour and eggs with a tad of water and a dash of salt, then mix and knead until it was perfect. Then she would roll the dough out into giant circles that took up an entire double-size bed. These sheets would sit on the beds for a few hours until it was time to return to the kitchen. Grandma rolled the sheet into a log precisely 2" wide. And then, with lightning speed, she sliced that log into ¼" pieces. When all the sheets were rolled and cut, they would be unrolled and dusted with flour while they awaited being cooked for dinner. What a wonderful time it was to watch her cut that roll. There were always tiny end cuts that would not make it to the pot because we kids were sitting there eating them raw. They were a great snack before dinner!

On the stovetop was a giant pot of tomato sauce. Grandma made her sauce from her garden tomatoes. In the sauce were things some people would never imagine eating—beef neck bones and oxtails, sometimes snails. We all grew using these ingredients, and to this day, I still include them in my canned sauce. Well, maybe not the snails so much anymore. I wish I had had more patience to create a sauce using real tomatoes.

I remember Grandma handpicking the tomatoes she would use. She washed and quartered them and put them in a pot for stewing. As they cooked, she would filter out the skins and seeds. It took forever for the sauce the reach the point you could add a thickener and the spices and the meats for flavoring. The process from the garden to the table took days! When it was done and poured on top of that homemade pasta—well, there was nothing better in the world.

Grandma always served pasta from a giant breadboard. It covered the top of her kitchen table. The cooked pasta would be drained and poured onto this board, where she added some sauce and plated the meal. She would let us kids sprinkle the parmesan cheese on top of each plate. We kids loved to sit around the table and eat strands of pasta right from the breadboard. No dishes were required for our

CHAPTER 2 | TRADITIONS

dining pleasure—eating from the breadboard was reward in itself. How I cherish the memories served up at that table!

One day I was introduced to the magic of the hand crank pasta maker. You make your dough and run it through several levels to make it thin and fabulous. Then you ran it through the cutter. As great as this was, it tired out your cranking arm in no time at all. Volunteers to crank did not last long. I made pasta this way for years. It was a small slice of heaven, so much better than store-bought from a box. Somehow, I felt I was carrying on my grandmother's tradition of homemade pasta. After all, it was her recipe. I still use her recipe today, but I now have adapters for my stand mixer—no more cranking handles for me. I will still make my ultra-thin pasta sheets and lay them on flour sack towels on my kitchen table to air dry before cutting them. After cutting, the pasta will hang on a drying rack until it's time to cook. I wish I knew what happened to the giant breadboard. I wish I had it. I would love to throw my cooked noodles on it, add my sauce and cheese and grab a fork.

My mother and her sisters all knew how to make sauce from garden tomatoes. I had never bothered to learn that method, as it took forever to cook them down, strain them, and everything else that went with it. I did have a wonderful recipe using canned tomatoes, and the resulting sauce came pretty close to theirs. With my recipe, I could create a pot of magic in a matter of hours before adding my secret ingredients.

I always loved making pasta for dinner parties. My husband always insisted on the "good sauce with oxtails" when he wanted to impress guests. He loved to brag to people that I cooked my sauce for days and days until the oxtail was so tender it was softer than filet mignon. This was a pretty funny thing for him. When we first started dating, I invited him to my place for dinner—pasta with oxtail sauce. He took one look at the oxtail and turned his nose up at it. He had never seen nor had oxtail before. He was not going to eat "that" unless I told him what it was. I said, "Try it. You will like it." We almost broke up that night. He eventually tried and fell in love with oxtail, and it became his favorite.

Growing up, I spent a lot of time with my aunt. We both loved experimenting in the kitchen. Unlike my great-aunt, who had all her recipes in her head, this aunt loved to write them down. I would vacation at her home just to spend time with her in the kitchen. We could spend an entire day just reading through cookbooks checking out recipes. I cannot tell you how many recipe books she has just on biscotti. No matter how many we checked out, the family recipe was always my winner.

Together we made cakes, cookies, and candy. We always had a wonderful time making cherished memories. She taught me how to decorate cakes, making them into masterpieces with little effort. She was like me—measured everything and followed the recipe instructions—til it came to the sauce. She could make the sauce as grandma did.

A week before my aunt died, I visited her. When I returned home, I made a pot of my "cheater sauce," as she called it. While making the noodles, I heard her tell me that I needed to make pasta for her family. She passed the day before my scheduled return, but I gathered my pasta equipment and

CHAPTER 2 | TRADITIONS

stowed my roller and cutter in my carry-on bag. I got through airport security with no problems at all.

The next day I went to make the sauce and discovered we were lacking the primary ingredients. While I prepared a shopping list, my cousin went out to the freezer and returned with a giant tub of homemade sauce from garden tomatoes. I added some ground sausage and a few extra cans of tomato sauce and let it simmer until the entire house filled with a magical aroma. The pasta was made and hung on the rack to dry.

Little did we know how amazing this dinner would be—our grandmother's recipe for sauce and pasta on the table at the same time. I could not remember the last time that had occurred in my adult life. We were all so busy that no one had time to make this meal from scratch anymore.

That night, everyone around the table felt the presence of my aunt. She was enjoying the meal with us as we toasted her and celebrated her extraordinary life. There were hardly any leftovers, which is very unusual for an Italian household. It seems that I did not make enough food. Leftover pasta was always excellent the next day. What little that was left was consumed for breakfast the following day by my daughter.

The next time I made pasta and sauce at home, my daughter commented that it did not hold a candle to Aunt Ann's, even as good as mine was, "Boy, mom, you should have learned how to make that sauce." She was right. I should have learned how to make the sauce—no one left to teach me now.

Amongst the cherished souvenirs from my aunt is her recipe box—a collection of fabulous foods from everywhere. Recipes that the local grocery stores handed out, some from the backs of product boxes and many from sugar and flour bags. They were a little something from "here and there," and there was some genuinely fantastic stuff in this box. Some even came with memories of our trying them over the years.

One thing my mother taught me was how to make meatballs. Back in the day, all the ingredients were added to the mixing bowl and mixed by hand. I always use lean hamburger meat, not that fatty stuff. Lean was better, so you would not get greasy sauce when adding the meatballs to the sauce. I use fresh eggs, seasoned Italian breadcrumbs, a bit of whole milk, salt and pepper, and of course, parmesan cheese. Hands were double washed and dried before being allowed in the mixing bowl. As a child, I thought mixing raw eggs in with the meat was a cool thing; as a teenager, I wished for a pair of gloves before mixing the eggs in. Now, I understand how much faster and easier it is to mix everything by hand. Let me wash my hands and dive right in. Mom always kept her hands wet while rolling the meat into a ball. I never gave it a second thought until I was teaching my daughter how to make meatballs. The recipe was correct, but they did not look the same. They were missing something. I watched her for a bit, and it suddenly hit me. Her hands were dry. After a quick lesson in wet hands, she re-rolled each meatball in wet hands, and they were magically perfect. Mom's recipe has since been updated, going from frying to baking, but they taste as

CHAPTER 2 | TRADITIONS

terrific as always. They still simmer in the sauce for an afternoon, sharing their favor with the tomatoes. Yum!

There is some tradition or knowledge of something that does not pass from generation to generation in every family. It does not matter if it is how to sew, meal planning, crocheting, knitting, embroidery, or other skills people in your family can do that another cannot. My great aunt's daughter was wise enough to realize that we all have that special recipe we are famous for that no one else in the family makes. A recipe we got from our mothers and grandmothers. She lovingly put together a fantastic family cookbook of all those recipes. When she brought me a surprise copy, she sadly smiled and said she regretted not having her aunt, my grandmother's, easy scratch recipe for pasta. Boy, was she happy when I pulled out a pen and paper and wrote it down from memory! She quickly printed up a page for the book and sent a copy out to everyone.

Along with the famous pasta recipe is the generations-old biscotti recipe. The same one my mother made for family parties and funerals. The torch has been passed to me to bake these dishes for family occasions.

When my mother passed, it fell to me to make the biscotti for her funeral reception. There was so much going on in my kitchen that night that I made them using one wrong ingredient. Mom very nicely sent me a sign the following day telling me to toss that batch and create a new one—and do not screw them up this time! My first time at the helm, and I messed up, but it was also the last time I messed up her cookies. Today I can make them perfectly from memory. Mom has never had a reason to complain again.

The cookbook encompasses many family's worth of great times. My grandmother was one of six; my mother was one of 11. Add to that the number of children my grandmother's siblings had, and all that they had. It is a boatload of family recipes created over the years, each with a cherished memory of enjoyment and happy taste buds.

Luckily, the family recipes will not disappear as long as the book exists, and we pass it from mother to daughter or son. I have added many new recipes to it over the years; I hope my daughter and granddaughter will cherish it long after I am gone.

Chapter Three

The Wisdom Within
By AJ Cavanagh

AJ Cavanagh

AJ Cavanagh is an intuitive channel who learned of his psychic and intuitive abilities while growing up in Australia.

Together with his husband Thomas Workman, they channel "The Guides"—native elders, extraterrestrial beings, ascended masters, angels, and elementals. These Divine beings share messages of Source Consciousness on the expansion of joy in body, mind, and spirit.

AJ and Thomas can help you attune to the wisdom within to help you connect with the larger knowing in the Universe and for you to create a more intentional and joyous life.

Visit www.SpeakingfromSource.com to contact AJ, book a private channeling session, or add your email to our Wisdom Wednesday club to receive free inspirational messages from The Guides.

The Wisdom Within

By AJ Cavanagh

How do we find wisdom? When I was a child, I considered my parents, who seemed to have wisdom in abundance, a key source. They had most, if not all, of the answers to my "But why?" questions. It's easy then to assume that wisdom comes from learning from others, and in part, it does. Now well into adulthood, I can attest to that myself. I've learned many things through my life experience, like knowing when the right time was to leave home, travel abroad, start a new career, and when to buy my first home.

But I knew there was another factor involved. There exists another aspect that I had become aware of, even back when I was a child. And this other factor is one I had been secretly cultivating, strengthening, and practicing for several years.

I realized that there was a kind of wisdom *within* me. It appeared at the most random times, but I was able to recognize it, and it was not something external to me. It was my own inner-knowing, my intuition. When I was a child, not a lot was made about the topic of intuition, but I came to the realization that my intuition was so much more than just good luck, a hunch, or gut instinct. Somehow, I knew that I was my own receiver of wisdom. This knowledge didn't come from my mind, but something deeper, eternal—divine.

CHAPTER 3 | THE WISDOM WITHIN

This wisdom has come to me in many varied ways—sometimes a whisper and sometimes a shout—and I realized it varied by how open I was to receive it. I remember this happening with the realization at an early age that I wanted to live overseas. As a young boy coming of age in Australia in the 1980s, it seemed there was a whole world to discover away from the vast island continent on which I was born. There was nothing wrong with Australia of course; it just seemed like I was living in the country, and I wanted to live in the city. And when the opportunity came by way of a one-year work exchange visa for Canada, I took it. I was 23, and as I've often said, "I left home, and I left the country." It was a big move for me then to be pretty much self-supporting at that age with mum and dad a whole hemisphere away. But I also knew then, deep inside, that the transfer would not be a temporary one but permanent. And it was. I've loved returning to visit Australia over the years but have equally loved living in North America. Today, another desert is home—this one in Phoenix, Arizona.

That early experience of being on my own and relying on instinct and intuition got me thinking that the source of my wisdom was more than just my sensitivity, but a connection to Universal Source Consciousness itself. I developed a reliance on this awareness, and it has never steered me wrong but has often frightened me with prospects leading me into the uncharted and unfamiliar, pushing me to trust, learn, and grow. Like the time I became fixated on an area of Phoenix that I'd never been to before. I kept being drawn up there, far north of the city center, close to a rock formation called "The Boulders" where the city of

Scottsdale meets the town of Carefree. Once, it was to buy a bookshelf I had spotted for sale online, and another time I was lured up that way to check out an estate sale. So, I guess it would be no surprise to you if I said the home where I write these words is also in this same area. According to the wisdom I was receiving, this was where I was meant to be, at least for now. Something had been coaxing me there. Perhaps my positive energy for the area triggered the law of attraction? But more likely, the Divine knew the location of my new home all along and, so too, my happiness here.

One of the joys I have discovered walking the spiritual path for many years is a gradual "lifting of the veil" from what was once unknown to what is now becoming known. This lifting of the veil, so to speak, begins with learning of the self. This often starts with thinking about some of the big questions, such as "Why we are here," and "What are my purpose and intended path?" For many, the answering of these questions can take a lifetime or even several lifetimes. However, the fun part of this journey is finding an understanding beyond the self. Here, you discover that you are not only from Universal Source but a unique and necessary aspect of it. You hold the answers to many of these big questions and the so-called secrets of the Universe, as you are part of it, rather than separate from it.

For some, we call this a discovery of consciousness. Often believing we are separate and alone, through going within, we realize we are part of everyone and everything—we are part of a sophisticated planetary ecosystem. Through connecting to our higher self, we learn how important everything is around us—the trees, plants, and animals—

CHAPTER 3 | THE WISDOM WITHIN

right down to the air we breathe, the rocks we walk on, and the water we drink. Being connected in this way is a wonderful discovery that each and every one of us can make.

But there is more still. There is our connectedness and relationship to the entire Universe. Yes, the Universe itself holds immense knowledge that we can tap into and access for ourselves. My quest to understand wisdom has led me to realize that it is not found externally from others around us or even separate from us, as in a belief in God or a higher power. It comes from this understanding that we are an aspect of source and the divine itself.

Together with my husband as intuitive channels, it's been thrilling to open to receive the many pearls of wisdom found in Universal Consciousness. A growing number of individuals are now receiving wisdom directly from the Universe through a wide range of non-physical, inter-dimensional, and intergalactic beings.

For several years, my husband and I have received wisdom from a collection of entities we call "The Guides." The greatest wisdom we have received from The Guides is the need for us and all of humanity to correct our belief that we are separate from the higher realms and that the divine beings we worship hold exclusive domain as the wisdom keepers rather than ourselves. The message The Guides have repeated to us and our audiences in many ways and on many occasions is that we are not separate from Universal wisdom.

We are, in fact, a divine aspect and purposeful part of creation. Many, like myself, will first shake their heads and say "No—this is not what my culture or religion has taught me. We are simply meek and mortal beings, and we are not intended for such higher knowing. How is it possible that we could be the wisdom keepers of the secrets of the Universe?" Well, I don't expect you to believe me. But just read what we have channeled from The Guides on the matter:

The divine has many opportunities to decide how it shall express itself—in the human body, in a different dimension, or on a distant planet or system. You can look at a campfire and see the many popping embers that shoot out around from the source of the fire itself. This is a beautiful way of thinking about souls and the divine energy of their origin.

We are not separate from the wisdom of the Universe. We are embers from the divine source itself, with all of the ability for love, awareness, understanding, and insight as source itself, to the extent that our human capacity and physical dimension in the 3-D realm permits. As an intrepid astronomer and science advocate, Carl Sagan once wrote:

The cosmos is within us. We are made of star-stuff. We are a way for the Universe to know itself.

The apparent separation occurs when we do not allow ourselves to be open and receptive to this aspect of Universal Consciousness. This seems particularly true right now, as we are experiencing the tumult of discovering more about who we are, our role on the planet, and our relationship to it. It's not quite so easy—as we tune into the evening news, the many struggles we face are quickly apparent. But going within, rather than lashing out at others, or bemoaning our circumstances, is the key to

CHAPTER 3 | THE WISDOM WITHIN

learning that we are the wisdom keepers ourselves. We hold knowledge. We hold answers. We have hope, and we welcome the future. The Guides speak again about this:

Clear yourself to enjoy the moment and become one in the moment. As you do so, a new dimensional access to consciousness will occur for you to access a higher reality and awareness. Each discovery you make, each understanding, each realization and connection you find all combine to the wonderful light of Universal Consciousness.

Is it no mistake that those we consider to be enlightened or spiritual first advise the seeker to learn contemplation, self-reflection and then ultimately take up the practice of meditation? It is often only in becoming still—becoming quiet—that we can take a moment to hear what our higher self is willing to share. To tune into the wisdom of our guides or ancestors so that we may grow our understanding or, at the very least, find inspiration from the magical insights that Universal Consciousness has to share.

Looking externally and following others—those who are your role models, political leaders, or popular on social media—and by enjoying the physical things you covet, can bring joy and some level of satisfaction or even understanding. Still, following this path is like choosing the long road to enlightenment. There is, of course, nothing wrong with any of that. But through meditation, there is an opportunity for you to recognize that you are your own wisdom keeper, and this is how to truly get on the fast track of enlightenment. For many, this is happening right now as an unfoldment of consciousness is being experienced among individuals worldwide. The Guides speak again:

We would encourage you to recognize the seed within all the human endeavors that is divine. It is in everything. It is in everything that you do. It is in your food; it is in the way in which you care for your pets. It is in every single thing that you do, to some degree. You cannot help it, for it is who you are. It is what you are.

Today's leading philosophers and scientists are just beginning to understand that consciousness permeates reality. This, the great sages of time have always known. Rather than being an exclusive trait of the subjective human experience, an awareness of consciousness is now considered a foundation of the Universe, present in every particle and all physical matter. It seems absurd to be living here on Mother Earth, with all of the wonderful things provided here for us to enjoy, and not to recognize the omnipresent consciousness. We are just now starting to learn and appreciate Gaia as communicating wisdom in multiple ways – through rocks, crystals, and the frequencies of the Earth itself. And as Earth beings, we are part of that wisdom. There is consciousness in everything. Just look around. The Guides again:

We often see ourselves as separate. Separate from the earth. Different from the animals, the plants, the water, and the rocks. And sometimes, even separate from each other. Yet, we all share the part of creation from the divine. We all have that within us—connecting us.

In 2004 a landmark book became a worldwide best-seller. Its author, Masaru Emoto, claimed that human consciousness could affect the molecular structure of water. His book, *The Hidden Messages in Water*, showed photos

CHAPTER 3 | THE WISDOM WITHIN

of the difference in ice crystals formed in water subjected to positive thoughts (intentions), words (prayers), and sounds (vibrations). It showed that water, and indeed entire oceans, serve as a receptacle to hold planetary consciousness.

Researchers at the University of Southampton's Optoelectronics Research Centre have recently managed to record and retrieve five-dimensional digital data using, of all things, a quartz crystal. Crystals have long been associated with sages and the new-age community alike for their ability to hold and store vibrations, similar to how Masaru Emoto discovered water did in 2004. And yet, a more simplified way of looking at crystals is knowing that they are, essentially, pretty rocks. Now science is harnessing the properties of these pretty rocks to create a quartz crystal disc capable of storing the data equivalent in 22,000 iPhones. By slightly changing the way light travels through the crystal, scientists can create polarization to enable the data to be read similarly to how we use fiber optics today. How about that!

The native ancestors of our lands have long honored the Grandfather and Grandmother stones held sacred in our mountains, hills, and valleys. They have several sacred ceremonies through dance and music, which enable them to tap into this Universal wisdom. But perhaps more obvious in our popular culture today, is the idea of the "Crystal Skulls" as holding sacred knowledge that can only be read or understood by sages and mystics. In November of 2020, I was honored to be a channel for the collective consciousness of the Crystal Skulls—known as the

WISDOM KEEPERS

Wisdom Keepers themselves—and this is part of what they had to say:

We are here to represent all of humanity. We are a conduit for all humankind. A conduit of ascension so that you may understand the universal mind. Use us to access the universal mind as you attempt to do when you bring us together to unlock the creative forces of the collective knowledge between us.

Know that this is what you are to do for yourselves as well. There is knowing in the Universal Mind. There is understanding in the collective. We have come forward at this time because you are able and ready to receive.

The Crystal Skulls remind us in their crystal purity to open ourselves as clear receivers—to still our mind in order to become clear channels of consciousness itself, just as they are. Significantly, the Crystal Skulls are intentionally modeled in our image so that we may recognize that nothing separates us, and we ourselves can hold such knowledge. There is no coincidence in this fact.

The divine is in everything. The water, the rocks, your next-door neighbor, and your beloved pet. And yes, even the Crystal Skulls. We are all aspects of the divine. We are all the wisdom keepers of consciousness.

Messages from The Guides tell us now that this is the time for humanity to accept a deeper understanding of who we are and recognize the wisdom residing within each of us. Before, we knew wisdom from a mental perspective. But now, we are coming to a realization of wisdom from a cellular perspective—wisdom that resides within us at the cellular level, deep and enduring.

CHAPTER 3 | THE WISDOM WITHIN

But why now? Why is it now important to go into meditation, step into the present moment, and discover this aspect of ourselves as an aspect of the divine and consciousness itself? Perhaps because, in a way, we are the last to recognize this aspect. We are the last to realize who we are and our place in the Universe. It may well be that the plants and the trees know it. It may well be that our beloved pets and the many animals in the wild know it. Almost certainly, Mother Earth—Gaia herself—is aware, ascending, and evolving to a new, collective higher consciousness vibration. For us, knowing our wisdom represents our natural and inevitable evolution.

And so now is the time for us to consciously enter this new age of knowing and partake of this new Earth. The growing pains are being experienced right now by a great many on this planet. This is a time of great change, and part of that change is discovering the wisdom within. We are the key to our own evolution. Our ascension does not come from government, a higher deity, or even from visitations of our galactic friends. It comes from being open to receiving and discovering our own nature as divine beings and sharing in the wisdom of Universal consciousness.

As we come to this new consciousness, many will discover remarkable abilities, insight, and understandings. It may be quite overwhelming, but now is the time to prepare by opening yourself to meditation and living in the present moment. The past can only offer you so much wisdom. The future has yet to be created. The present moment is where it's at and where you will discover the answers you seek. The Guides offer this to lead us forward:

WISDOM KEEPERS

Make your wishes constantly known. Daydream often Imagine what you wish to create. Now is the time to envision life without limitations.

However, many of us have been taught to believe that our wishes are no more than fairy tales. We think we have to earn our blessings through hard work or rely on pure luck to get what we want. But The Guides remind us that our desire and our trust in the Universe does result in manifestation. The more we focus and allow, the more we realize our dreams. The Guides here also tell us that *now* is the time to dream and create freely and see what you are capable of manifesting. As our knowledge of who we are expands, The Guides promise that our ability to manifest will grow as well. We just need to make a wish and then to keep on wishing!

Good luck on your journey, Wisdom Keeper. Remember, you hold all the ability to discover who you are and connect with source consciousness. You get to choose your experience—a stressful journey full of anxiety perhaps, or an exciting one full of wellness and abundance. You decide. And if you do not like what you have decided, then you can choose again in the present moment. It's that easy, and it's that magical.

There is a new connection to oneness coming to Earth and affecting the entire consciousness of everything and everyone. As you read this, you may not possibly imagine the wisdom you hold as a divine being or the wisdom you are about to unlock with this realization. But do as The Guides tell us, be open to receiving and keep dreaming.

Chapter Four

'Tis The Season:
A Holy Day Rant
By Anne Foster Angelou

Anne Foster Angelou

Anne Foster Angelou lives in Seattle, WA, with her native-born Greek husband of 47 years, Dimitri. She has been retired since 2007 from her government employment as a Records Management Analyst and after 20 years as a professional member of Seattle Opera's resident chorus. She founded the Angelou Vocal Ensemble, an a cappella quartet, that performed in private venues for holidays and special occasions until 2012. Her other pursuits included a Certificate in Private Investigation and training as a Master Home Environmentalist (volunteer) for the American Lung Association of WA. Anne remains curious about life, loves cats and enjoys the accomplishments of others. She is a loving, encouraging and supportive friend, an avid reader, and enjoys humor and laughter. Learning is lifelong, and wisdom is to be shared. Anne is grateful for everyone who has ever entered her life.

Email: fosterangelou@comcast.net

'Tis The Season: A Holy Day Rant
By Anne Foster Angelou

Greek tradition says Καλό Μήνα (good month) on the first day of each month. Happy December 1st. May your month be a good one. This is an intense time for me and many for whom the holy days are not merry. Is it S.A.D. or deprivation of light and the descent of darkness? Its regular recurrence every year would seem to say so. Is it COVID and the radical changing of the world as we know it?

The world is hurting, and ignoring it or pretending otherwise is not helpful. *The Power of Now* book suggests concentrating on the present moment, which is all we have, they say. We draw to us what we think. Do we? Other wisdom says depression comes from thinking about what has happened and giving it a meaning, a painful one, a discouragement, and that anxiety is about dwelling on the future and fear of what might happen.

Scarlett O'Hara would say, "I'll think about that Tamarrah!" or "fiddle dee dee!" when she didn't agree or didn't want to face something.

As a human being, I assume that many think and feel as I do. How do others feel when they are repeatedly reminded in the media of murders and other manifestations of violence, sexual, psychological and physical abuse, cheating, stealing, racial and economic injustice, and a myriad of human-caused atrocities. One can say it began in

CHAPTER 4 | 'TIS THE SEASON: A HOLY DAY RANT

the Bible with the Garden of Eden "story" when Cain killed Abel and when Eve ate of the fruit of good and evil.

Reverend Tom, in a Unity column, was asked, "Do you believe in the devil?" His answer: "I don't know about a creature with a long pointed tail and a pitchfork, but I do know that at the center of every atrocity is at least one human being."

Aside from "Acts of God (natural disasters)," humans cause nearly everything else. Why are they hell-bent on destroying themselves and the earth? We all contribute in large or small ways. Peace, love, forgiveness? These are solutions but not usually the first choice.

Why can't we see the "divine" in each other? Some do and make better choices. Many don't, and all hell breaks loose.

Expectations get us into trouble often. The "holy days" are a perfect example. The insanity has started the day after Thanksgiving—*Black Friday!* Buy, consume, spend on things that will never bring you happiness. Go into debt, and the things you shower on others will never convince them that you love them, and they will want more. No, I am not a grinch or Scrooge shouting, "Bah, humbug!"

Father Tim, a Catholic priest in our local parish, says he prays to want what he already has. We are so blessed but still complaining. I donated to charities that touch my heart, and I'm not done. "It is in giving that we receive" and that doesn't mean material things. I am blessed to have been born into poverty, want and deprivation that taught me what it's like to be on the other side of abundance.

My maternal grandmother, who raised me, made Christmas magical for me. She would find a leftover tree on the lot after the vendors had gone home on Christmas Eve. In the 50s, they didn't throw them into a grinder if they couldn't get the last dollar out of a last-minute shopper. She had collected decorations over the years and had a tradition of putting up a bare tree with nothing else in sight. To my delight, when I woke up in the early morning, the tree was decorated, and presents were underneath. Where she hid them, I will never know. Yes, we were poor and often the food we ate on holidays was given to us by charities. She managed to buy a few things for me: a doll, a board game, some clothing. Later, when I was a teenager, she would allow me to open one gift before going to midnight Mass and the rest in the morning. We walked a few miles each way to church.

The most beautiful part about Christmas is the music and lights. I can't imagine not going to church either. As a child, I sat on Santa's lap and probably asked for something politely. Wonderful gifts came from England from Granny Foster, my father's mother, things not found in the U.S., or so I thought.

My ex-husband, rest his troubled soul, loved Christmas, according to his sister. In our brief marriage of seven years (mostly apart), I remember he loved to give books or practical items like books of stamps. He would put fictional character names on the gift tags like Rudolph, Santa and once, Simon (Oliver Reed's character), a psychotic killer from a movie we had seen recently. I didn't think it was funny.

CHAPTER 4 | 'TIS THE SEASON: A HOLY DAY RANT

Happiness is not in things. It takes a lifetime to realize that. Still, I have had expectations for many years and such anxiety that I couldn't bring myself to buy a tree and, if I did, I would fall asleep with it lying on the floor, undecorated. I need a shrink. I have drawers full of beautiful Christmas cards, increasing in volume year by year with various denominations of stamps to go with them. They remain unsent. I have the best of intentions. I love handwritten communication and dread receiving a pre-printed card with just a name, no personal message. Why bother. I know who you are, I know your name, and you could have saved the postage. Judgment! Shame on me.

My husband of 47 years says it's not his tradition to give gifts on schedule, on a holiday. He has given me amazing gifts and not for any particular occasion—18K gold filigree matching necklace and earrings with emeralds, a gold Byzantine cross with an emerald, a pair of Byzantine earrings with sapphires, rubies and gold granulation (tiny beads on the surface). After my heart surgery, he began to give me flowers or plants (orchids). When we first met, he bought me dresses or things for the house (bedding, kitchen items). He isn't a person who expects or wants gifts. God bless him!

The holy days also remind me of hunger and lack of necessities, even though it's been many years since I have been in need. This time of year reminds me of the homeless, those without medical care, food, clothing, living in so much pain. For those who have homes, a now-deceased poet friend once said, "Do you realize how lonely people are? They are kissing their television sets, the characters on the screen."

I hear it starts with me. I can make the world a better place. I can change my thoughts and continue to act with love and generosity. I can change my tears to smiles and laughter if I just see the good all around me and fill my mind and heart with gratitude. I can change fear to hope and calm. I'm trying. In this COVID isolation, masking, distancing, thank God I have a loving spouse for affection and companionship. It's easy to live in fear of losing each other, of what might happen economically. I am not wallowing in self-pity, but we have no family in the U.S., and holy days are for celebration and togetherness. As loving as we are and appreciative of each other, we are quick-tempered and argue about so many things. Luckily, we quickly seek forgiveness and mending.

I am not accepting of what is, and I'm engaging in repetitive review about past and long-ago pain of separation and loss. The little child in me and the "fixer" wants it to be all better no matter how long it's been. Wisdom has taught me that I am only responsible for my own behavior and choices, not anyone else's. Nevertheless, I will blame and torture myself with guilt. Some will end relationships in the most painful way with shunning, ghosting and pretending you no longer exist, even people who were full of loving words and generosity and after years of what you thought was an endearing and lasting friendship. A psychiatrist told me in my 20s, when I was facing my divorce and suffering depression, that losing a person to death is far easier than losing a living person when it's their choice to leave you behind. It's true.

CHAPTER 4 | 'TIS THE SEASON: A HOLY DAY RANT

I'm so impressed to hear of separation that is amiable and done in the most loving way possible, for the good of all concerned. It can be done.

I researched shunning and learned that it is the angriest, most vindictive pain to inflict on another when it is done in retaliation for a perceived real or imagined hurt. It is also passive-aggressive. Humans make mistakes, sometimes awful ones, and the worst can be forgiven. The pope forgave his would-be assassin. I read about a family whose son was killed by another young man who was driving while drunk. The guy was so remorseful and was forgiven by the parents and became a second son to them. Jesus said, "Father forgive them, for they know not what they do." Jesus also said, "I do not say to you seven times, but seventy times seven." Matt. 18:21-22.

Dimitri says I have a loving and forgiving heart, and that's true. I have an active conscience and accept accountability for my mistakes. I am much more likely to care about others before myself. I am learning to work on self-love, and it's not easy.

What does any of this have to do with "Wisdom Keepers?" I am the recipient of wisdom from years of trial and error and deciding what feels right in every circumstance. I had trouble with the "keepers" part of wisdom because we must share, give it away, and let it be there for the taking. I am grateful for all those who taught me what they know. I hope my voluntarily acquired wisdom is of use to others. I have so many opinions about life because they feel right for me. As Oprah says, "what I know for sure" is that love, generosity and forgiveness are the solutions, the healers.

We are one and cannot survive in this life without each other. We need humans, animals and the earth. Our animal friends are angels on earth and teach us unconditional love. The earth is our home, giving us fresh air to breathe from the beautiful, life-giving trees, soil to grow our food and solid ground on which to build our homes. We have life-saving water to drink. Please love our precious, sacred Mother Earth. Do not poison her with chemicals. Stop fracking the mountains and find other less harmful ways to provide energy. Do not support GMO or Franken Food. Vote with your dollars. If you don't buy it, they will give in to supply and demand and not sell what is not fit for human consumption (or one would hope).

Our world is full of human greed and a lust for power. Yes, humans are responsible, and we can decide we are "mad as hell and not going to take it anymore." Don't be a part of it. Vote with your conscience and put your money where your mouth is. You have a choice of where to bank. Do a little research and find a financial institution with a conscience. Credit unions are often more ethical. Check them out.

Honor your temple. Feed it nourishing food, exercise. We are one of the most obese countries in the world and the richest. Humans are hurting spiritually, emotionally and then physically. We must support a government that works for the people and not for their own gain. We need term limits. If they are good enough for the POTUS, they are good enough for our legislature.

Demand that they work for the citizens of this once great country. My wisdom tells me that we are in this together, and everyone must have the basics to survive and thrive:

CHAPTER 4 | 'TIS THE SEASON: A HOLY DAY RANT

shelter, food, clothing, clean water, medical care and education. No one should suffer because of the color of their skin, a religious belief, who they love, a disability, or their sexual identity. Yes, I want to strive for an ideal world. I don't want to give up even though the daily local and worldwide news frightens me with the violence of war, discrimination, and animosity and antagonism among individuals. I am terrified by police violence but encouraged and feel safe because of dedicated men and women of conscience who work for law enforcement.

I don't want to hear of another shooting, not another atrocity caused by humans. It hurts too much. We must be the change we wish to see in the world (Gandhi). We must also do our best to seek the truth about everything as much as possible. I am unvaccinated, a personal choice based on my health conditions and four risk factors for COVID. I am not a conspiracy theorist, a Trump supporter or an uncaring or crazy person. I am a proponent of natural, complementary and alternative medicine in addition to what conventional allopathic providers have to offer. I am never passive in my medical decisions.

Wisdom Keepers? Share your wisdom, don't keep it to yourself. I am not finished learning and will continue as long as I draw a breath. There is so much more to know, so many more decisions to make for the benefit of all living beings.

With all this seriousness, I forgot to mention one of my most favorite things: laughter, being goofy, finding humor in most things. Have fun!

Remember that we humans make mistakes. There is no perfect person. Forgive someone and make two people happy. Be grateful every day for everything. This is my wisdom. I hope it helps. There's a cartoon birthday card with the Dalai Lama on the front holding an empty box. He says, "Just what I've always wanted, nothing."

Be well, safe and happy. Happiness is not what we have, our accomplishments, our credentials, or who we know. It's all about love. Make the world a better place. You won't regret it.

Chapter Five

Learning to Quit
By Karen Gabler

Karen Gabler

Karen Gabler is an attorney, intuitive mentor and psychic medium. She is passionate about assisting others with a wide range of emotional and spiritual transitions, guiding them to lead their most productive and fulfilling lives. Karen works with her clients to provide intuitive guidance regarding their personal and business questions, developing strategies to help them overcome obstacles and manifest their highest purpose. She also conducts intuitive readings for clients and facilitates connections with their loved ones in spirit.

Karen is an international best-selling author and inspirational speaker. She conducts seminars and workshops on a variety of spiritual, business and personal development topics. She taught transcendental meditation as an assistant teacher in Hawaii and legal courses as an adjunct law professor in California.

Karen earned her Bachelor of Science in psychology and her Juris Doctorate from the University of Hawaii. She is a WCIT in Martha Beck's Wayfinder Life Coach Training program and has pursued wide-ranging education in interpersonal development and the spiritual sciences, working with tutors from the prestigious Arthur Findlay College for the Psychic Sciences in England, as well as with intuitive coaches and psychic mediums throughout the United States. Karen has participated in more than thirty workshops and mentorships on metaphysical topics and intuitive coaching.

Karen enjoys reading, horseback riding and spending time with her family.

You can find Karen at www.karengabler.com.

Learning to Quit
By Karen Gabler

The air was crisp and cool with the chill of impending winter in the air. I saddled my horse, Shiloh, for our Saturday morning lesson as he danced from side to side in the cross ties. "You're feeling bright today, aren't you, boy?" I murmured to him as I patted his neck. I swung my leg over the saddle at the mounting block, and we stepped into a ring filled with jumps. As I gently squeezed my legs around his girth, my typically-lazy Thoroughbred took off like a shot, trotting as fast as his legs would carry him.

My trainer, Wendy, was clearly in a dark mood as she wrapped a blanket around her shoulders and barked orders at my fellow barn mates in the ring and me. After twenty minutes of exercise at walk, trot and canter, it was time to begin our jumping practice. Wendy set rails in a tiny "x" formation and told us to trot over them to warm up. As Shiloh caught sight of the jump in our path, he suddenly charged forward, clearing the one-foot cross rails by at least two feet.

"I told you to trot it quietly!" yelled Wendy.

"I know you did, but he's definitely not quiet today!"

"Do it again!"

I circled the ring and pointed Shiloh toward the little jump once more. He began pulling me toward it, straining at the

CHAPTER 5 | LEARNING TO QUIT

bit in his mouth. As he landed on the back side of the jump, he tossed his head and began hopping across the ground. I felt a bolt of nerves shoot through me as I struggled to regain control.

"Do it again!" yelled Wendy.

"Wendy, I don't think we should jump anything else right now. He's really on fire today!"

Wendy threw her hands up in frustration. "He's not going to do anything bad! Just hold onto your reins and sit up. Do it again!"

As I hesitated, Shiloh began prancing in place, pulling the reins out of my hands. I repeated my concern: "Wendy, I really don't think it's a good idea to jump today. I don't feel comfortable sitting on him right now."

I saw the anger flash in Wendy's eyes. "Fine! Just quit! Get off right now. Your lesson is over!" She called to one of our more experienced riders standing at the fence. "Yvonne, take Shiloh from Karen and get on him. You can jump him today." I wordlessly handed over the reins and stepped back, feeling my cheeks redden from the embarrassment as much as the wind. I felt like a chastened child, afraid to ride my own horse and being punished for quitting with a kindergarten-era time out.

Yvonne mounted Shiloh and trotted off around the circle. As she approached the little "x" jump, Shiloh again began to lunge toward it. Yvonne pulled on the reins to slow him down as he continued to drag her to the fence. He leaped over the tiny jump, again clearing it by several feet. As he landed on the other side, his head dropped to his knees and his back legs kicked out into a thunderous buck. Yvonne was launched into the air, landing hard on her hip. She lay on her side in the ring footing with the wind knocked out of her, gasping for breath. Shiloh took off at a gallop around the ring, bucking and hopping. As I passed Wendy on my way to catch my horse at the other end of the ring, I swallowed the words on the tip of my tongue: "*I told you so!*"

Legendary football coach Vince Lombardi famously said, "Quitters never win, and winners never quit." We are taught from childhood that quitting is shameful. When I "quit" riding my horse that day, the clear implication in my trainer's frustration was that I just didn't have what it took to fight through adversity, to dig deep, to search for success. I was given no credit for self-preservation or for understanding what was right for me in that moment. Although I stood up for myself in choosing not to push forward with a squirrelly horse, I did so out of fear—tentatively, haltingly, as if I was asking for permission to take care of myself rather than making the decision that was right for me.

In *The Word Detective,* columnist Evan Morris reports that the word "quit" came from the Latin noun "quies," which means "sleep, rest, repose, absence of activity, absence of noise, freedom from disturbance, freedom from anxiety, placidness, serenity, tranquility, peaceful conditions." This definition supports the true meaning of quit—to achieve freedom, peace, rest. To leave something that no longer serves you and to prioritize your personal needs rather than what others might expect of you. It was not until the industrial revolution that the word quit began to be used to

CHAPTER 5 | LEARNING TO QUIT

represent an absence of productivity, as in "to quit a job." When our self-esteem and perceived value became tied to our tangible output, we stopped focusing on who we were *being* and instead began focusing on what we were *doing*. As the accomplishments of the day became more important than health and happiness, popular opinion began to assert that the word *quitter* was synonymous with *loser*.

Recent events have finally begun to create a much-needed shift in this societal perception. During the Covid-19 pandemic, management professor Anthony Klotz coined the term "The Great Resignation" to describe the tidal wave of employees choosing to quit their jobs rather than return to the workplace. After months of pandemic stress and uncertainty, thousands of people reassessed their priorities. Many decided to resign from their employment positions, choosing to retire early or pursue alternative careers with better work-life balance and personal fulfillment. The U.S. Bureau of Labor Statistics reported that more than four million people quit their jobs in July of 2021 alone. Analysts have offered a variety of explanations for this mass exodus, but experts agree that disillusionment and lack of fulfillment are key drivers. Whether this has arisen from rampant fear about health risks and longevity, or merely a long-awaited opportunity to hit the pause button, the fact remains that society is reckoning with the effects of the last five to ten decades and looking for a new way of life.

To be able to refocus our lives and pursue a more fulfilling future, we must revise our perceptions about what it means to let go and reframe our language around the concept of quitting. Quitting can mean that we have finally let go of something that wasn't working for us. It also can mean that we've let someone else down or let ourselves down. And yet, even when we "let someone down," aren't we doing so because we are engaging in self-care in some way? Aren't we placing our own needs above those of others—and shouldn't we strive to do exactly that? In the book, *Impossible is Stupid*, author Osayi Osar-Emokpae said, "Quitting is not giving up; it's choosing to focus your attention on something more important. Quitting is not losing confidence; it's realizing that there are more valuable ways you can spend your time. Quitting is not making excuses; it's learning to be more productive, efficient and effective instead. Quitting is letting go of things (or people) that are sucking the life out of you so you can do more things that will bring you strength."

Even when we are firmly committed to quitting, it remains important to refocus our language to reflect exactly what we are quitting. After a somewhat alarming health checkup, I pondered years of yo-yo dieting and lamented my lack of success. I realized that my on-again, off-again commitment to quitting a variety of my favorite food items was typically short-lived. "I'm quitting chocolate! I'm quitting pasta! I'm quitting chips!" I would stay firmly "on plan" for at least a day or two, and sometimes even up to a week—only to quickly tire of the restrictions and quit the diet. I realized that if I wanted to remain motivated to improve my health, I would need to reframe my description of exactly what I was quitting. I started by making a list of the things I truly wanted to quit: my lack of energy, the pain in my joints, the struggle to find something to wear, the lack of quality sleep, my inability to go on a long hike with my family. I wanted to quit feeling depleted and dejected. I wanted to quit feeling like a failure. When I refocused my goals on what I truly needed or wanted to quit in order to live my best life, instead of dwelling on what I wasn't "allowed" to put in my mouth, I began to feel empowered and strong. I began to find satisfaction in small gains, and the things I chose not to eat became secondary to the joy I felt at being able to run up the stairs without gasping for breath or walking on the beach while on vacation with my family.

Sometimes, our reluctance to quit is based upon concern over the amount of time or money we have already invested into a particular relationship or activity. Behavioral science research describes the *sunk cost fallacy* as our tendency to insist on following through with an endeavor if we have already invested time, effort or money into it, whether or not the current costs outweigh the benefits (or lack thereof). We forget that throwing even more time or money into something that doesn't work for us will never allow us to recapture what we've already lost and, in fact, will cause us to lose even more in the future. Author Aubrey de Graf said, "Don't cling to a mistake just because you spent years making it." It is important to consider whether it makes sense to invest further time or money in something that hasn't worked in our favor thus far. Rather than asking whether there is a way to recoup our past investment, we must instead ask whether this endeavor is worth our future investment. Will staying in place serve the person we want to be? Will it lead us to the things we want to do?

Because we have been conditioned to see quitting as a negative, we tend to describe the end of a relationship or the loss of a job as having failed in some way. Too often, this prevents us from embracing the opportunities newly available to us after a significant change in our lives. If a relationship ends in divorce, are we required to feel only the sadness or anger that it didn't work out? Or can we learn to see it as an opportunity for both parties to find a more meaningful partnership or move toward their next phase of growth? If we are terminated from a job, does it have to be devastating that we no longer work for that company? Or can we find a way to take advantage of the freedom to pursue something more fulfilling or chart a different course for our future? Losing something we wanted—or, at least, something we thought we wanted—can be painful, to be sure. That doesn't mean that it must always be painful or can only be painful, and it doesn't mean that we can't find the gift or the growth in an unexpected life shift.

To be able to move toward a more productive future, we also must take control of our own lives and our own decisions. We are in charge of our choices, even when we feel like the victim. In a struggling marriage, for example, we might dwell in rage or hurt at what someone else has done to us. *How could they act like that? Don't they know how much they are hurting me? Why would they do this to me?* In fact, aren't we doing it to ourselves? Aren't we responsible for our own decisions in life? In a marriage counseling session prior to the end of my first marriage, I railed at the therapist. "Aren't you supposed to be helping to make this better? It doesn't seem like you are helping us make any progress toward fixing this! None of his behaviors have changed at all!" She put down her pen and looked at me carefully. "I'm not here to fix you or to fix

CHAPTER 5 | LEARNING TO QUIT

him. It seems to me that he has been very clear about who he is and what he will or won't do. The only remaining question for you is whether you want to keep living this way or whether you want to make a change." I was stunned into silence, recognizing the wisdom in her words. Indeed, my ex-husband wasn't doing anything to me—I was doing it to myself by remaining in place. If I wanted to live my life differently, I would have to take steps toward the life I wanted to live. Once I was able to see that I alone held the power to decide the course of my life, I was able to let go of the feeling that it would be "wrong" to quit my marriage and then open the doors to a relationship that would fill my soul and allow me to grow as a person. Our joy, our peace, our happiness, is always our responsibility.

When we are thinking of quitting something in our lives, it can be scary to think of stepping into the unknown. We wonder whether quitting is the right thing to do—are we giving up something stable in favor of something tenuous? And yet, if we choose to stay in an unfulfilling environment rather than leaving to pursue our passions, aren't we quitting on ourselves? Aren't we quitting on our hopes and dreams? Aren't we giving up our chance of fulfilling our purpose in the most joyous manner possible? In fact, when faced with the decision of whether to quit something, the choice isn't really whether or not to quit that particular thing. Instead, we are always faced with the choice of *which thing to quit.* Do we want to quit what we are currently doing, or do we want to quit on that little voice burning inside of us that tells us that there must be something more, something else to pursue with our one glorious life?

Throughout my legal education, I was consistently reminded that the appropriate path to a private law career was to intern in a law firm during summer breaks from law school, obtain a permanent offer as an associate at your chosen firm, rise through the ranks to partnership in the firm, then someday (if you were lucky), open your own firm. I followed the mold as described, ultimately opening my own law firm in the summer of 2011. After almost five years of running my own firm, when I should have been excited and happy about my accomplishments, I realized that I was mostly frustrated, tired and dejected. Despite my best efforts, the demands of running a business consistently took precedence over my legal services. Instead of helping clients to move their businesses forward, I was buried in administrative duties. I worked twice as many hours and made half as much money. I wondered why I wasn't overjoyed to have reached the pinnacle of my career and questioned my lack of gratitude for my success.

When an unexpected opportunity arose to sell my interest in my firm to my law partner, I initially panicked at the thought that I could be giving up everything I had worked so hard to achieve for so many years. Was I actually thinking of quitting my own law firm? What if I regretted it? Friends and colleagues told me I would be crazy to do it. Why on earth would I want to give up the right to chart my own course and lead my own team? Despite the constant pressure to remain entrenched in the success story I had always been told to achieve, I trusted my growing recognition that the life I had been told to want was not the life I wanted to live. After signing the agreement to give up my ownership in the business, I realized that I didn't quit

CHAPTER 5 | LEARNING TO QUIT

my law career at all. Instead, I quit dealing with paperwork, business obligations, financial decisions and employee issues. I quit being exhausted and working twelve-hour days. I quit working every weekend to catch up. I was able to return to my own legal practice and focused on client service and legal strategy, where I had always thrived. By quitting the burdens of running a business, I regained my desire to help others solve problems and the free time to pursue my own interests and connect with my family. I realized that in choosing to quit running my own law firm, I stopped quitting the rest of my life.

Sometimes, it can be difficult to determine whether we merely want to quit because pushing through our roadblocks feels too difficult or because quitting is truly the right decision for us. To determine if quitting is motivated by our fear or our desire, we must consider whether we are running *from* something or running *toward* something. Does this decision support our best life? Does it move us toward our higher purpose? We can more fully assess our reaction to a potential decision by pausing to feel the impact of that decision within our own bodies. When I imagine my life in this way, does it feel peaceful in my body? Joyful? Restful? Or, does it feel painful? Full of regret? Panicked? We must look at who we want to be in the world and then consider whether the choices we are making today will hold us back or move us toward the person we want to be. Author Annie Dillard famously said, "How we spend our days is, of course, how we spend our lives." Making a change in the way we live our lives or revising the way we view ourselves requires that we choose to quit what could be hundreds of day-to-day thoughts and actions that keep us anchored to our present reality so that we can explore an alternative reality that would be better aligned with our life path and purpose.

Ultimately, the willingness to quit, even when we have no idea what will come next, can be the utmost form of self-care. Rather than bowing to societal expectations, family pressures or feelings of guilt and obligation, we find a way to stand in our power and announce to the world that *this is not right for me, and I deserve better than this.* Author Elizabeth Gilbert said, "Everyone who ever changed their life or laid claim to their own destiny began by surrendering to two words: *not this."* Whether we are refusing to put ourselves in danger, running from a toxic relationship, leaving a soul-crushing job position, or simply saying "no" to the daily demands society places upon us, the art of quitting is the key to living our best lives. The choice we face in every moment of every day is not *whether* to quit but *what* to quit. Will we quit something outside of ourselves or quit on our own hearts? When we firmly commit to quitting everything else before we ever quit on ourselves, we realize the truth: quitters aren't losers after all. In fact, the beautiful, freeing truth is that quitters always win—and winners always quit.

Chapter Six

This Little Light of Mine
By Sarah Gabler

Sarah Gabler

Sarah Gabler is 15 years old and in the tenth grade. She loves playing games with her family and traveling to new places. Sarah enjoys playing the ukulele and guitar, singing and dancing, and riding her horse. As a lifelong artist, she is pursuing a scholastic pathway in visual art and loves using creative outlets to express her artistic vision. She is a technical sound artist for her high school productions and enjoys helping to bring a production to life to entertain others. She loves empowering people by helping them to recognize their true potential in the world and plans to do motivational speaking in the future.

Sarah began exploring spiritual teachings and soul empowerment concepts when she was ten years old and believes it has made her a better person today. It also has motivated her to find ways to live her best life and to help others on their journey to live their best lives as well. Sarah believes that even the smallest act of kindness can make someone's day, and she enjoys going out of her way to make others feel loved.

This Little Light of Mine
By Sarah Gabler

Nanea Hoffman said, "You can't control how other people receive your energy. Anything you do or say gets filtered through the lens of whatever they are going through at that moment, which is not about you. Just keep doing your thing with as much integrity and love as possible." This is a lesson that I have worked on and learned a lot about in the past few years.

As a sensitive empath, I have picked up other people's energy throughout my life. Sometimes, when I am picking up negative energy, I assume that it is directed toward me. I find myself constantly asking people if they are okay when I can feel negativity in the air because I feel like they are mad at me or they are upset about something related to me. I have learned along the way that there is so much more happening in people's lives underneath the surface than we may realize.

When I was in sixth grade, my best friend and I were attached at the hip. We met when we went to the same after-school club and became closer throughout the year. We spent almost all our time with each other. While we waited for our parents to pick us up, we would do our homework and other activities together. We had deep conversations about how we were feeling. We laughed a lot. I would always look forward to seeing her after school.

CHAPTER 6 | THIS LITTLE LIGHT OF MINE

When we began seventh grade, things began to change. My best friend would randomly become angry at what seemed like the smallest things. When she didn't understand a homework problem, she would lash out at me and push me away, even after I tried to help her. She would huff and puff in frustration and then bury her face in her hands. I asked her what was wrong, but she would just say, "Nothing!" She was too tired and annoyed to do anything fun with me. As the year progressed, she would go into these crazy tailspins, spiraling so much that it was hard to be around her. She would snap and yell at me or ignore me entirely. For the rest of the year, I constantly thought that she was mad at me but just didn't want to tell me why. I assumed that she didn't want to be best friends with me anymore, which made me really sad and angry.

After months of ups and downs in our relationship, we were sitting at our usual homework table one afternoon. Once again, she was snapping at me. All of a sudden, she broke down crying. I didn't know what to do! I patted her arm and sat quietly next to her as she sobbed. When her outburst subsided, she finally began to talk to me. She told me that her parents were divorcing, and her father was moving out. She then quietly shared that her father had been physically abusing her mother for the past year. She and her little brother had to hide in their rooms behind locked doors while their parents argued, hearing the cruel words and physical violence going on in the living room. It was only after her mother finally called the police that her father was removed from the house.

This shocking story certainly explained a lot of her anger and her resentment toward the world. I was stunned, realizing that this horrible scene was playing out in her life while I assumed that she just didn't want to be my friend any longer. Her behavior actually had nothing to do with me! I was just taking in her negative energy throughout the year and automatically thinking it was directed at me. My inability to separate her feelings from my own prevented me from seeing that something far bigger was going on in her life. Once I understood what was happening in her life, I was able to separate my energy from hers and just be there for her without worrying that her attitude was about me.

This experience allowed me to begin realizing that when you detach the behavior of others from your self-consciousness, you can release the stress in your body and be available to help others get through their difficulties, keeping an open mind and sharing your wisdom and support as needed. It taught me the importance of separating my energy from that of others so that I can stand in my power and be there for my friends and loved ones. There is so much good that you can do for yourself and others if you switch your mindset.

Despite this newfound awareness, however, I continued to struggle with assuming that others' negativity was directed at me. When I was 15 years old and in my sophomore year in high school, I took a class on creating the school yearbook. I was so excited to take the knowledge I had learned in my graphic design classes the prior year and channel it into a new venture, where I would be able to contribute toward a book that would hold a year of memories for my fellow students. I believed that the project

CHAPTER 6 | THIS LITTLE LIGHT OF MINE

would be a fun collaboration and really wanted to have a joyful class during my school day.

In the first few weeks of yearbook class, we worked to develop a theme for the book. After a year and a half of living through the Covid-19 pandemic, we were ready to leap out of our socially-distanced bubble and enter the real world again. I came up with the word "emergence" as a theme and title for our yearbook, acknowledging the feeling of being back on campus after a year of online learning. After a lot of debate, the class ultimately decided that they loved the emergence theme and agreed to build the entire yearbook around my concept. I was over the moon with excitement! I was so happy, knowing that it was less than a month into the class, and I was already making valuable contributions to the project. I was invested in making this yearbook as great as it could be!

To facilitate communication with the yearbook team, we used a messaging app called, "Remind." This app allowed the owner of the chat to contact and send messages to the rest of the class. Instead of my teacher being in charge of this chain, he allowed his teacher's assistant, a senior student, to run the chat and make sure everyone was on task. As someone who likes to be organized and stay on track, I was happy that the teacher's assistant would be sending out reminders about deadlines or tips for good writing. Unfortunately, that communication deteriorated very quickly.

A month into the year and a day away from our first deadline, we received our first deadline message on Remind from the teacher's assistant. It said, "All pages need to be done by *today*. A few of your captions and quotes are not good and stop using exclamation points! What the hell? If they aren't done, then your grades will look nasty. Our teacher already has names, and you know I told him details."

The tone of the message was shocking to most of the class. Since I had already turned in my yearbook pages, and being the sensitive person that I am, I automatically assumed that the message was directed at me. I was sure that the teacher's assistant hated my work and was expressing her anger at me. I responded to her message, explaining the work I had already submitted and defending myself. Naturally, this made her more frustrated and turned her attention directly to me, even if the original message had been directed at others. As soon as I turned in my edited pages once again, we received another Remind message that said, "I just wanted you to know that you still had captions and quotes that I didn't like, so I rewrote them. Next time, this won't happen. This was the last and only free pass you're gonna get!"

Coming on the heels of my submission, I was even more sure that this was all about me! As I became more stressed, I decided that the teacher's assistant clearly had something against me. I was upset by the nasty tone in her message, but I also was hurt that she didn't just ask me privately to re-write my pages and guide me by telling me how I could improve. I was positive that she hated me. I hadn't asked for a "free pass," and I was frustrated that I still had no idea what I had done wrong. As I kept spinning in my feelings, it never even occurred to me that perhaps the message wasn't about me at all.

CHAPTER 6 | THIS LITTLE LIGHT OF MINE

In yearbook class the next day, I anticipated a long lecture about why my yearbook captions and quotes were deficient, and I prepared myself for a detailed diatribe about why I needed to work harder on my writing. I was prepared to stand up for myself, and I was ready with rehearsed arguments and comebacks, explaining that I never did anything to her and that I was sick of being labeled the "slacker" of the group. To my surprise, when I walked into class that day, she didn't even notice me. Instead, the teacher's assistant was holding her head in her hands and staring at her phone. Several of her close friends huddled around her, whispering. Suddenly, she ran out of the room crying.

I later learned that she was crying because people were trying to spread rumors that she was "easy" and always willing to have sex with the boys in her classes. This had been going on for several weeks, and the taunts had escalated from the occasional whispered rumors to open sneering and laughter when she walked by others in the hallway. As I reflected on how she must be feeling about this bullying behavior, I realized that her attitude and harsh language toward the class had nothing to do with a grudge toward me, and the tone in her communications likely resulted from personal stress rather than feelings of hatred toward me or my fellow students. Instead, she was projecting her pain onto our class, and I was taking it in as my own. Once again, I was struck by a new perspective on why people might behave badly when they are struggling in their own lives. I suddenly felt more sympathetic toward her and forgiving of her negative behavior. Although personal traumas don't excuse poor conduct, I did have a better understanding of why she was acting so harshly toward us and a reminder that someone else's bad behavior isn't my responsibility. I received another little reminder that just because someone else's energy is negative or toxic doesn't mean they are mad at me or that I've done something wrong.

In mulling over that experience, I realized how much my false assumptions were impacting my own self-esteem. I began exploring ways to separate the energy of others from my own energy. I wanted to find a way to stand strong in my own space without allowing anyone else to impact my feelings. In exploring this area, I have discovered a number of helpful tools to preserve my own mental health and inner peace.

In a twice-weekly "free period" at school, I began writing weekly journal entries to myself. I wrote about anything that came to mind without a specific theme or plan of action. It might be about how I was feeling that week, or some drama that I needed to get off my chest, or anything else that struck me in the moment. This *stream of consciousness* journaling has helped me tremendously. I find that the more I write about how someone has been acting toward me and how I have been taking it in, the more I realize which part of it is truly mine and which part should be released. I am able to give myself advice as I think about the words spilling onto the page. I have begun looking forward to my free period every week so that I can write about how I am feeling. It has really helped me get my thoughts in order and separate my own energy from that of others. It clears my head and makes me feel more at peace and stable within myself and my surroundings.

CHAPTER 6 | THIS LITTLE LIGHT OF MINE

Another clearing technique I have tried with great success has been nightly meditation. I recently was given a Hatch sleep machine for my birthday. The Hatch allows you to set up a bedtime routine to help you achieve the most effective sleep each night. My personal routine includes a guided meditation where I am able to lay in my bed, relax my body, and clear my mind of the day's troubles and worries. This has allowed me to go to sleep with a calm and clear mind. I have found that instead of lying in bed and dwelling about everything that happened during the day, I can just climb into bed, breathe and relax. It makes my bed feel more like a safe and restful place instead of a place to wind myself up with the dramas of the day.

I also have found it useful to practice breathing exercises. It sounds like a simple thing, but just spending two or three minutes on deep breathing can significantly change my mindset. I take a deep breath for a count of four, I hold my breath for another count of four, then I release my breath slowly, using another count of four. By doing this several times over a few minutes, I can actually adjust my physical sensations, calm myself and clear my mind. I feel refreshed, balanced, and grounded in my own energy instead of being pulled around by others.

I also have practiced setting a specific intention to clear my energy from moment to moment throughout my day. When I suddenly feel like everyone is against me, I take a deep breath and say, "I pull my energy back to me, and send [that person's] energy back to [them]." Doing this helps to separate my energy from someone else's energy, and I can reevaluate whether the situation at hand is really about me or needs to be released from my own energy field. Along with sending another person's energy back to them, I remind myself that the person who is putting out negative vibes is just going through struggles in their own life, and they aren't thinking about me. This allows me to consider whether I can be helpful to them or whether I simply need to release the energy they are putting out into the world from my own body to make sure I am embedded in my own space and not allowing their energy to jump into my bubble.

When you are taking in negativity from others, life can be exhausting. You are constantly worrying about whether someone is mad at you, or you are feeling guilty or allowing your own mood to be dictated by the behavior of others. This can lead you to waste your own energy on false feelings when those feelings aren't actually yours and don't have anything to do with your life. After consciously separating your energy from others, you will feel like a weight has been lifted off your shoulders, and you will maintain a much lighter and more positive vibe throughout the day. When you do encounter struggles in your life (as everyone does!), you will have resources available to take you through the tough times, rather than depleting yourself with feelings that have nothing to do with you. Most of all, when you remain strong and clear within your own energy, you are able to be there for others without blurring the lines between you and them. Energy is powerful, and when you understand how to preserve and use your energy effectively, you can expand your light in the world and inspire others to do the same.

Chapter Seven

Reflections for Everyday Life
By Jaime Lee Garcia

Jaime Lee Garcia

Jaime Lee Garcia has been a Certified Law of Attraction Practitioner, through the Global Sciences Foundation, since 2015 and is also studying to become certified in *Belief Energy Clearing*. Jaime loves to inspire others through inspirational blogs and writing, has a passion for seeing people truly happy, and aspires to teach others the law of attraction principles which helped manifest great things into her life. Jaime would like to thank her family and friends for their constant love and support, as they bless her life in many ways. This chapter is dedicated to her beautiful Mom, Lora Judd, who never stops fighting the battle, has taught Jaime to preserve in life no matter the hardships, to make as many memories with our tribe as possible, and most of all, to love big.

You can reach her by email at secretwayoflife@yahoo.com or Facebook @secretwayoflife.

Reflections for Everyday Life
By Jaime Lee Garcia

"Mom, what's wrong?" I asked as my mom entered my office one morning with worry on her face and blood coming out of her ear. She had already been through so much, from breast cancer to metastatic breast cancer, which spread to her bones, and more health issues brought on by the disease and side effects of medicines. However, one would never know the battle she faces by looking at her. She is very youthful for her 76 years and always keeps busy, despite the cancer that is found in traces throughout her body, from her skull down to her thigh. Despite these obstacles, she trudges through each day with little complaint and is a true warrior. I tried to remain calm as I saw her panic when she mentioned needing to get to the doctor. Thankfully, it turned out to be something minor, although this does not prevent me from worrying over her when moments like this present themselves.

This woman has been my sidekick all of my life and my true inspiration. I feel it the highest honor that she decided to retire as a hairdresser in California and join me in Tennessee three years ago. I love that I am here for her in this chapter of her life and that I can savor many moments together, making more precious memories to cherish.

Every day, as I look at my mom, childhood memories surface and bring me back to many family holidays and special life events where she was right by my side. I am so

CHAPTER 7 | REFLECTIONS FOR EVERYDAY LIFE

thankful for the life lessons she has taught me by her leading example and also by her mistakes. Her words of wisdom shared with me over the years often come to my mind during everyday life, and I am very blessed that she's still here to continue to teach me. She is the reason I am a giver, a woman who loves unconditionally, has a passion for inspirational writing and reminding others what's truly important in life. My wish is to combine everything my mom has taught me, along with lessons I have learned along the way, to leave a legacy behind for my loved ones to learn from and be blessed with.

I would like to share some of these reflections so that you may reference them when going through stressful times in your life, when you need to be reminded of your many blessings, or even when you need a change of perspective.

- ♥ Practice gratitude. Before getting out of bed each morning, take a few moments to give thanks for the many blessings in your life, and you will be setting the frequency for more blessings to follow. This can be tough if going through challenging times but start with the fact that you woke up and have another day to share with your tribe. Be thankful for the heart that keeps beating because it means you're alive. Each day you are blessed to wake up, you are given a clean slate and another chance to change your path or pursue your passions. Another example is simply giving thanks for the roof over your head or the beautiful day shining through your windows. Believe me, there is always something to be thankful for, so focus on gratitude.

- Practice the same ritual when going to sleep at night. Give thanks for everything good that happened during the day, even if it's as simple as appreciating the comfy bed you get to slumber in for the next eight hours. If you had an awful day, replay the events in your mind the way you wish they would have turned out. If your boss was unbearable, create the image that he instead showed you validation and appreciation. If you woke up late and had to rush to make it to work on time, replay the day as if you woke up with plenty of time to get ready, had a moment to stop at Starbucks for your favorite Mocha Frappuccino, and made it to work with breathing room to spare. While doing this ritual, you're setting the right frequency for more blessings to come. Remember, gratitude equals blessings.

- When life gets overwhelming, and you're stressed to the max, practicing self-care is vital. Create a tranquil environment by diffusing an uplifting essential oil, lighting some candles, turning on your favorite music, creating art, or sitting outside to enjoy the sounds of nature. Learn the practice of meditation and deep breathing. Take time for yourself each day. After all, you serve others the majority of every day, whether at work or taking care of the family.

- Travel often. It's easy to stay in the comfort of our bubble, but seeing the world and different cultures

CHAPTER 7 | REFLECTIONS FOR EVERYDAY LIFE

enriches our lives and gives us amazing experiences and memories.

- ♥ You are who you hang around with, so surround yourself with people who lift you and inspire you to be your best version.

- ♥ Be someone who lifts others up and makes them believe in the goodness of people.

- ♥ If you're a leader, make sure you're leading people in the right direction. If you're a follower, make sure you're following those who represent the values you want to encompass.

- ♥ Every day, you have the choice to make decisions that lead you closer to the light or farther away from it. Always choose the light, and don't forget to be the light for others.

- ♥ Quit being your worst critic and start celebrating everything that makes you unique. We are not in this life to compete with others, so stop trying to measure up. Everyone is born with strengths, weaknesses, talents and gifts. Instead of focusing on what you think your faults are, celebrate your strengths and everything positive and good in yourself. We evolve with time, so be patient with yourself and be your biggest fan.

- ♥ We all have broken pieces and can feel damaged from time to time. This is life and it is based on our experiences. We cannot escape hardship, but we can choose how we react to it. Learn from the hard times and grow from them. It's only then that you can be your own warrior.

- ♥ It doesn't matter how far you've traveled down the wrong path. Learn from the decisions that brought you to those crossroads, but don't let them define you. No matter how bad life seems at a given moment, you have the power to change your life. Everything starts with a thought. If you want to change your life, then you have to change the way you think. A healthy life starts with a healthy mind. Who do you want to become? What impact do you want to make on this world? It's all within your power.

- ♥ Lead your life with compassion, kindness, and gratitude, and let love be the driving force behind all you do. Also, remember to spread it upon each person you touch.

- ♥ Love yourself more than anyone else can. When you love yourself, disappointment and hurt from others will not cause such a huge hit because you will know your true worth.

- ♥ Everything happens for a reason, so stop with regrets. Every good and bad thing that has happened to you are life lessons, which are valuable to our growth, so learn from them.

- ♥ Don't forget to live while you're alive. We are here for a short period of time. Life goes by way too fast and does not stop at a certain age. So, if you find you want to learn how to play the guitar at 70 years old, then do it. You are never too old or too young to give something new a try.

- ♥ Don't rush through each day without seeing the beauty around you. We are here for more than just work and chores. So, remember to stop and appreciate the world around you. Look at the pretty blue sky above you and the gorgeous flowers blooming during the spring. Enjoy the beauty that each of the four seasons brings. Take a moment each day to look at the loving face of the child you created and brought into this world. Let their laughter fill your heart. There are many beautiful things around you, so don't forget to pause and take it all in.

- ♥ Read books often. We stop growing when we stop learning. Books are filled with stories, valuable lessons, and they can take you away to places you've never been. Enrich yourself.

- ♥ Find your passions, and you will find your purpose. There is no time limit to this. We evolve and change with each phase and decade of our lives. Therefore, quit being so hard on yourself to get everything figured out by a certain time.

- ♥ Celebrate every moment of your life. Most people dread turning a year older each year. Look at it differently, as birthdays are good for you. The more you have, the longer you live. So instead of cringing, celebrate the years that you have been gracing this earth and wish for many more to come.

- ♥ You are never too old to make a wish on a candle each birthday or on a coin before you toss it into a fountain. Wishes can and do come true.

- ♥ Spending time connecting with nature is good for the soul. It's been said that grounding is very healing on your body. This means taking off your shoes and planting your bare feet on solid ground. Take a barefoot walk on the grass, letting the soil soak into your skin. You can even sit in a chair and place your bare feet in the grass. You will find when doing this, your stress level reduces, and you're bringing peace and healing to your body and soul.

- ♥ Take pride in every space you occupy, as it's a direct reflection of you. This includes your house, your car, bedroom, or office space. What do people see when they enter your space, and what does your environment say about you?

- ♥ Family is everything, and family comes first. Although we cannot choose the family we are born into, we can choose friends who also become family. Cherish these amazing people because they are your tribe.

- ♥ Our loved ones are often taken from us too soon and sometimes without a goodbye. It's vital that you love and validate your tribe every moment you get. My dad and brother were taken from us unexpectedly. There is no way to protect the soul from the grief that hits when we lose the people we love, especially when it's sudden and without warning. I had thought that I could call my brother over the weekend when he came to my mind on a random Thursday night. He and I spent our lives being extremely close and connected. However, I got a call that Saturday morning, which instantly changed my life. My brother had been involved in a tragic accident the night before. There were to be no more calls between my brother and me. He was gone forever and without a goodbye. This was a devastating lesson to learn. Call your loved ones often. Do not let texted words on a screen maintain your relationships. Hearing your voice is a gift that is so precious to those that love you. I wish I could hear my dad's and brother's voices one more time. If you haven't talked to a loved one in a long time, pick up the phone. Time is precious and should not be wasted.

- ♥ Cherish your family traditions. There is nothing I love more than remembering all of the holiday traditions my family created together. When I miss them the most, and we are living far apart, these memories keep them close to my heart.

- ♥ Learn to be a giver and not a taker. Give with no expectation of receiving anything in return. There's no better feeling than giving and seeing the joy on another's face. I am not talking about spending a lot of money. I am talking about paying it forward with gifts from the heart. Something as simple as spreading your smile can go a long way and change a person's day around. Be a giver of love and joy and watch the domino effect take off.

- Do not let material things consume your life. Stay humble. It's great to have expensive things, but do not get too caught up in them. The perception of relating material items to success is a falsity. Success is not how big your house is or how fast your car drives. True success is who you are as a person and what you contribute to others and to the world. At the end of life, the only thing you can take with you is the love and memories you made here on earth with your loved ones.

- There's nothing better than cooking meals with friends and family, so put love into it. Everything tastes better with that very special ingredient. Many cherished memories are ones where loved ones are creating something amazing together for everyone to enjoy. Think about the smiles and laughter that surround the dinner table as everyone enjoys the ritual of sharing the amazing feast made with love.

- Let your kids help you cook. Not only does this teach them a valuable life skill, but you're building memories they will cherish forever, as well as passing down recipes that will stay in the family long after you're gone.

- Everything you do each day creates habits, good or bad. Pay attention to your daily habits, so you can make the changes needed for your better health.

- Never underestimate the power of a Hallmark movie and a cup of steaming hot chocolate, especially during Christmastime.

CHAPTER 7 | REFLECTIONS FOR EVERYDAY LIFE

- ♥ Spend time with children, as they teach us about true unconditional love. Children love others based on intuition and not conditions. I wrote a blog a few years back regarding a little boy I had met in my mom's hair salon. As he walked by where I was sitting, I had asked him about the toy he was holding in his hand. He never actually talked to me. He merely stared at me as I interacted with him, extending out his hand to show me what he was holding. After a few minutes, he skipped off in the direction of his family. When the time came for them to leave the salon, I smiled at him and told him to have a good night. He turned to his mother and said, "I love her," as he skipped out the door. I was shocked hearing his words because he never actually spoke to me. I realized then that his words of love were based on his pure intuition and not on a condition of time. We adults could surely change the world by loving so unconditionally.

- ♥ Do not let differences of opinion ruin your valuable relationships. I have seen family and friends stop talking over arguments of politics, religion, and the like. We live in an era of freedom of speech. It's okay to not agree on such topics. Agree to disagree and do not let these differences create division and hatred. It's simply not worth it. How boring would the world be if we all agreed on the same topics? We can learn and grow from each other if we keep an open mind.

- ♥ When it comes to your mate, it's important not to lose yourself in the relationship. A great match is when you have enough things in common to keep you bonded but also enough differences to learn from each other. You are both on this earth to live your individual lives, so don't lose sight of that. Balance is key between personal hobbies and time dedicated to your relationship. Do not let the scale tip greatly to one side or the other.

- ♥ Never feel stuck in a relationship. If it's not working for you anymore, do not settle, or both of you will waste precious years being miserable. It is okay to be on your own, especially if it means you're in a better place emotionally.

- ♥ Make your child your biggest investment, as they are your legacy. It's easy to get bogged down by all of the stresses and responsibilities of the day. Do not let your child feel like a burden you do not have time for. No matter how bad or busy the day is, practice patience and take the time to let your children know that they are loved and valued. Greet them with smiles, hugs, and love, as they can have tiring days just like us. Do not forget that you are their calm to the storm and their main source of security. Before rushing to make dinner or tend to household duties, spend a few moments to take an interest in their day. Show them value by giving them your time. Make it a nightly ritual to sit with them and read a book together or just simply talk. In doing so, you're creating precious memories together and helping boost their self-worth.

♥ Never think of yourself as a victim. Instead, keep in mind the survivor and warrior you are. Persevere and keep going. Life is filled with many challenges and tragedies, but it's also filled with many blessings and beautiful moments.

♥ Wherever life takes you, and no matter how far you go, if your current path does not suit you any longer, you can always go back.

♥ The light is always within you, so remember to ignite it during times of darkness.

♥ Sometimes you have to let go of things that are overwhelming or out of your control. I was always told to "sleep on it." Everything is usually better when the sun comes up, and there's great comfort in this.

♥ Life is defined by the moments we share with our tribe, so never take them for granted. When loved ones are gone from our lives, this is what we will have to keep them close to our hearts. We honor them by keeping these memories alive.

I give tremendous thanks to my mom for teaching me that the most valuable things in life involve family, great friends, and making precious memories to cherish. My wish is that my daughters and grandchildren will refer to these reflections and words of wisdom long after I am gone when they need gentle reminding of life's blessings and of how truly amazing and gifted they are.

WISDOM KEEPERS

To all of you reading this book, always celebrate the magnificent being you are. Believe in the magic of yourself, and always remember to "shine on."

Chapter Eight

Our Memories Sustain Us
By Patricia Holgate Haney

Patricia Holgate Haney

Patricia Holgate Haney has had a passion for travel since she jumped in the backseat of the family car on trips to "anywhere and nowhere." Inspired by her love of books passed down by her father, she immersed herself in the written word, which further sparked her interest in travel and writing.

She is an author, travel professional, ordained minister and paralegal. She has been published in four compilation books which are available at Amazon, Barnes and Noble and local bookstores, as well as her website, phtravels.com.

She and her husband Gary enjoy travel, cooking and spending time with their family, which includes two sons, three grandchildren and three great-grandchildren.

Proceeds from book sales at phtravels.com are dedicated to a monthly donation drive for the homeless, which she and Gary host monthly.

Reach her by e-mail at memories@phtravels.com,

https://www.amazon.com/author/patriciaholgatehaney

On Twitter and Instagram, find her at phtravels.

Our Memories Sustain Us
By Patricia Holgate Haney

I remember how I loved to take an old blanket and a book out to our front yard when the grass was ready to be mowed. The higher than usual grass slightly cushioned the blanket and I lay on my back, searching the skies.

I loved watching the patterns that birds made when they were together. Sometimes there was one leader; other times, there may be multiple lead birds. I wondered how they all found each other, and curiosity led me to read more about birds in my dad's Audubon books.

It was relaxing hearing the breeze blow through the trees nearby.

Occasionally the sound of a dog barking or the train in the distance added to the atmosphere.

It was fun to watch the clouds drift by, the speed determined by that day's wind. As they floated, they morphed into shapes of all kinds. When by myself, I tried to guess what they would be next and named them appropriate to what character they became.

Sometimes I'd be joined by a friend.

It was fun to play a version of I Spy with my friends where we shouted out to each other our best guess as to what shape it had become. We got creative at times, stripping pieces of white paperbark from the birch tree on the

CHAPTER 8 | OUR MEMORIES SUSTAIN US

property line and using it to write secret notes or draw before it fell apart.

If we wanted a snack, we had so many choices, we could go along the retaining wall to Mrs. White's strawberry patch and eat them right there, go around the corner and up the hill to a neighbor who had pomegranates—most of the time I felt they were too much trouble for what you ended up eating.

Oranges were everywhere, and on the street that led from the elementary school, there were kumquats and sometimes lemons.

Laying there, we snacked on fresh fruit from the nearby trees—apricots, plums, oranges; other times slurping up cold juicy slices of watermelon. It was, looking back, idyllic. For us, it was just playing.

There were orange groves and dairies in our neighborhood until development started happening as people moved out into what was considered the "boonies" and found affordable housing away from downtown areas of Los Angeles.

The San Gabriel mountains loomed in front of us. Sometimes capped with snow.

Even with changes, the clouds were always there to tweak our imaginations.

Cement rivers, known as irrigation ditches, meandered through some of the streets behind houses. Other houses butted up to dairy farms until new developments were built. The hills behind the housing tract held great fun for anyone who ventured up there. You could find cow skulls, meandering paths through thickets of grass, sometimes snakes, and other wildlife, including skunks and the occasional mountain lion.

We would romp through the hills, making up games. We trudged pieces of cardboard to the top of one of the hills, affectionately known as Cardboard Hill, and slid down.

Our moms would get together for coffee and sit and talk, watching out the windows at the activities. Helm's or Golden Crust Bakery trucks regularly visited the neighborhood, and kids rushed to pick out a treat. I loved the lemon tarts—next to my Mom's lemon meringue pie, they were my favorite dessert.

We always knew when the Good Humor man was coming through because the loud tunes from his truck announced his arrival. Kids scrambled for dines to buy their frozen treats. We waited in line impatiently, perusing the photos of goodies available that day—bomb pops, rainbow pops, orange-sicles, Eskimo pies, and more.

Each type of frozen confection had its own method of eating to avoid the inevitable melting, runny mess that dripped down our hands and arms, leaving sticky residue everywhere. Someone always had a hose in their yard or a sprinkler that provided the cleanup. Water fights ensued, and laughter filled the air.

Some families had regular dinner hours because their dads worked day shifts. A lot of us had dads who worked rotating shifts at either utility companies or factories. The number of the kids in the street varied with whose dad was home for dinner.

CHAPTER 8 | OUR MEMORIES SUSTAIN US

It's funny because I can still remember some of these things like it was yesterday. Sweet memories of the aromas that wafted through the neighborhood from dinners being cooked, orange blossoms in the air, and a few not so pleasant like the smell of the dairy when we were downwind or the incinerators burning garbage, even the occasional skunk who marked their territory or lost in a battle with a car.

I cherish the memories and the simple pleasures derived. As time went on and we grew up, many rushed through life and lost track of those simple pleasures. Some being drafted go to war in Vietnam. Others got caught up in the hippie movement, some went off to college, some, like me, got married young.

As new parents, the joy in holding a baby, warm and fresh from a bath, and the sound of giggles and cooing and later attempts to talk filled our days. We began the rushing through life, the simple joys there, but little time to enjoy as we made a living, found our places in life, and rushed through the days. The future seemed so far off. Little did we realize how precious these memories were to become.

Throw in events like divorces, custody battles, deaths of close family, moving to new places far away, and losing track of friends and yourself. The simple pleasures almost passed with insignificance. Yes, new memories were made, but it all seemed so complicated.

There were other turning points in the direction of life. First, my mom had cancer, then my dad. When Dad had his surgery, I remember how my consistently stoic mom seemed so scared. Only if you knew her would you have noticed. I decided I was not going to leave her side. I ensured my two boys were cared for when I wasn't there and sat by her side in the hospital for days, with only short trips home to check in.

I think that we became closer than we ever had at that time. Dad and I were always close, but I had never felt this close to my mom. The experience forged a new bond for us.

Dad had accrued so much unused sick time and vacation that he could take the time necessary to recover and then take early retirement. Needing and wanting a change, they moved to the foothills of San Diego.

I moved to Northern California, which meant there was even more distance between us. We visited back and forth, and the three of us took a memorable trip to the UK and Ireland. My dad was especially excited because we could see locations where he had researched and traced his heritage. It was so much fun watching him and the pure joy he was feeling. We went to Ireland and visited areas from where Mom's family had immigrated. Dad and I did a lot of whiskey tasting, which helped make the trip even more colorful. Some of those stories will remain untold.

A few years later, they decided to move elsewhere as the neighborhood they lived in had changed.

One weekend, I went for a drive as I tended to do to de-stress. I loved seeking new and exciting or unique places and exploring backroads. I was north of Sacramento and had seen some incredible history and towns in a guide and decided to wander. At one point, I drove through the town of Paradise.

CHAPTER 8 | OUR MEMORIES SUSTAIN US

Something hit me in the heart driving through. It was a small town, yet not too distant from larger cities. It was in the mountains with forests and rugged scenery. The places I stopped in town were quaint, and the people were generally friendly and welcoming. I immediately thought I needed to tell the folks about this place. It spoke to me, and I imagined them living there.

I took photos and sent them copies and a map. They were heading to Oregon to check out a place they had heard about and decided they would go through Paradise and check it out. Even the name seemed a perfect fit and sign.

They ended up buying a place in Paradise.

Their home was at the end of a cul-de-sac in a gated park with beautiful manufactured homes on spacious lots. A wrap-around deck overlooked a forest of trees and a meandering path that led to a pond. Deer and other wildlife wandered, and Mom used to update us on the new arrivals and could pretty much time when they'd show up. She knew exactly how many trees she could see from one spot in the kitchen and loved hearing the wind blow through the pines joined by the sound of birds calling out.

I remember walking the path below their house with Dad and sharing conversations about everything and nothing. We reveled in the beauty of the spot. Looking up the incline to their home, we saw Mom at the kitchen window watching over us as she did "her" trees and deer. A smile and a quick wave, and she went back to what she was doing. Dad smiled and said she was in her happy place.

They had indeed found their Paradise. Dad even set up their answering machine with a message that started, "For those who thought Doris would get to Paradise before me—"

They were taking time to enjoy the simple things. The signs of the season, the wildlife, the sounds of nature.

They enjoyed walks and hikes together in the surrounding area. They still traveled but felt that they were where they were meant to be.

Dad once again became an active member of the local genealogy center, helping people from around the nation and world. Mom made friends and enjoyed trips to the local casino with them, playing bingo and slots. She loved coming home with her winnings and "making it rain" for Dad, showering him with the winnings. He loved seeing her so happy, and he always laughed at her antics.

Then it happened.

First, Mom suffered severe heart conditions, and we almost lost her.

Then Dad began to fall, and his movements were becoming stiff.

Dad was diagnosed with Parkinson's, and it progressed quickly.

He ended up moving into a facility where they could give him the intense care he now required. It was around the corner, and Mom sat there with him every day.

Dad could use his computer for a while to do his research, but it became challenging, resulting in mood changes and

CHAPTER 8 | OUR MEMORIES SUSTAIN US

pessimism. After many trips and emergencies, it was apparent Dad would not be able to be at home any longer.

I had been transferred to Arizona, and we were flying back to California as often as we could to help. Finally, they made the tough decision to move to Arizona to be closer to my sister and me. It was not an easily made decision, as they loved their home in Paradise.

Things quickly progressed once they moved here. As his disease progressed, his communication was limited, and he could barely speak. Angry that he could not be understood, he became more despondent. He was incapable of doing anything for himself.

Mom was still able and wanted to live independently. Dad could not. Even though Mom had stopped driving, she made her way to Dad's side every day, rain or shine.

Dad passed a year after they moved to Arizona.

He had not wanted to be buried in the past, but as he got more involved with his genealogy, he decided he wanted to be cremated and then interned. We chose and had him interned in the historical Paradise Cemetery, a place he loved. We held a small memorial service, and all his friends and fellow researchers came and told stories about the mysteries he had solved and how much they admired him.

Mom and I talked at least once or twice a day, and we visited with her every weekend. While she was still able, we took her on little adventures, as she called them.

Drives to different places and bonus points if there was a casino, trees, and maybe a Frosty. I cherished the time we had. I began to look at each moment as I had when I was a kid looking at the clouds. Little phrases, physical traits, jokes, stories that, even though I felt I'd heard some of them a hundred times, became treasures. I was taking time to be. Be with her, be with the moment.

Mom passed six years after Dad. A few months before she died, we were on the phone together having a conversation that was both playful and serious. She was ready to go, she said; Mom felt she was not living.

At the end of the conversation, we agreed that she would give me a sign when she was around.

When Mom passed in 2012, our family took a portion of her ashes, walked the path to the trees in sight of her kitchen window, and spread them lovingly at the base. Each of us stood reflecting silently and occasionally making comments, and as usual, they were steeped in our family tradition; they were peppered with humor.

The balance of Mom's ashes joined Dad in the memorial niche. Inside was a laminated wedding photo of the two of them beaming.

My dear lifelong friend and sister of the heart, Janet, presented us with commemorative angel pins. Each had one with their birthstone. Both pins were lovingly placed in the niche. Our parents had been such close friends, and now they were all gone. My parents would have been touched by her loving gesture. We shared beautiful and humorous memories, laughing at the probable trouble they were getting into, including laughter, margaritas, and our moms admonishing our dads to behave.

CHAPTER 8 | OUR MEMORIES SUSTAIN US

They were together in Paradise, yes, but their memories lived on in my heart.

We receive signs from Mom often. There were signs that we might have missed if we weren't mindful and attuned but thank God we were. They have provided us with such a sense of peace.

In 2018, the Camp Fire destroyed the town of Paradise. My parent's home, along with over ninety percent of Paradise, was gone.

The genealogy library where Dad devoted time and took such great pride burned along with all the precious documents housed inside. A research room had been named for my Dad, and it was all lost. Friends died along with their homes, and the memories that filled them burned to the ground. Paradise was lost.

It was one time I was glad my parents had already passed. They had been interned in Paradise Cemetery, and I was filled with dread wondering what that meant to all the history there, as well as my parents.

In 2019, we took a road trip during Christmas and New Year with our youngest son through Northern California and visited Paradise.

None of us had been there since the fire. Driving up the hill from Chico, you could see the devastation. As we got closer to town, the smell of ashes permeated the December air even a year later. Chimneys and some burnt-out frames of cars were scattered throughout.

One or two homes were partially standing in different areas. Surrounded by burnt vegetation and various items bent from the heat and black with soot, it was apocalyptic.

A few businesses had tried to open, and the land was being slowly cleared, but it was heartbreaking.

We arrived at the entrance to the cul de sac where they had lived, and every single structure in their neighborhood and around it was burned.

With trepidation, we drove to the cemetery. All around the cemetery, structures and trees were burned to the ground. The little ramada where they had memorial events was even burned. We drove into the cemetery, and I kid you not, the fire had stopped about 10-20 feet from their internment spot! All three of us were stressed and anxious about visiting the cemetery, but we all exclaimed in surprise and then burst out half laughing, half crying. We could hear Mom saying, "You will not burn us out!"

Their final resting place might have been hot as hell, but it survived untouched.

When we take time to recognize and give thanks for the activities or events that seem minuscule at the time, we find that they occupy prominent places in our hearts.

I look to the sky, am aware of the beauty in the simplicity of clouds, and drink in the beauty of even the smallest plant or creature of nature every day. They seem to be mnemonics for memories that sometimes get tangled up in the rush of everyday life.

CHAPTER 8 | OUR MEMORIES SUSTAIN US

I sometimes worry as I get older that the memories will fade and be lost. That is one of the many reasons I started to journal.

"But watch out! Be careful never to forget what you have seen. Do not let these memories escape from your mind as long as you live! And be sure to pass them on to your children and grandchildren." Deuteronomy 4: (NLT)

Don't only make memories; protect your memories. They are precious and priceless. Those that seem insignificant at the time will sustain you.

What memories are you leaving for others?

Chapter Nine

Almost Home
By Marianne Hudspeth

Marianne Hudspeth

Marianne is a published author, naturopathic physician (ND), registered nurse, has a Masters in Written Communication from National-Lewis University in Chicago, is a Reiki master, observer/tester for Associate of Therapy Dogs, and she has made several medical mission trips to Haiti to deliver health care.

One of her passions is writing, so she has been a contributor to other compilation books

She strongly believes that Mr. Rogers' mom was right about "look for the helpers."

She is a helper.

She rides her own Harley-Davidson Sportster Touring and loves spreading love through humor. Her solo book "Empty Nest, Full Throttle 2" is a series of her adventures on her Harley-Davidson. It is an Amazon best seller and is available through Amazon. She has signed copies available at jimariahup@aol.com and jimariahup4@gmail.com.

She lives in Arizona and Mexico with her beloved, James Hudspeth.

Almost Home
By Marianne Hudspeth

Last night I finished watching the final episode of "The me you can't see." It's a series about mental health co-produced by Prince Harry and Oprah Winfrey. They had many international guests on their expert panel. I could relate to much of what was said when they discussed anxiety, depression, bipolar disease, schizophrenia, and suicide and how these and other mental health diagnoses can be caused by both trauma or DNA, or both. You know, nature versus nurture.

My family has a long history of anxiety, depression, abuse, suicide, and alcoholism. More on that later.

Then we adopted my son, who has bipolar disease with schizophrenic affect. We adopted him from Haiti when he was two years old from the Missionaries of Charity in Port-Au-Prince, Haiti. To do this, I spoke to Mother Teresa in about 1980. She was in Calcutta at the time, and when I spoke to her, she said they had no children available for adoption in Calcutta because the children there all had parents. These children were left with her when their parents were unable to care for them. Some of her children needed food because they were malnourished. Some were ill. When the children recovered, they would return to their parents.

Mother Teresa said that she would check with the motherhouse in Haiti because they likely had children

CHAPTER 9 | ALMOST HOME

available for adoption and that she would contact that house in Port-Au-Prince. Someone from there would contact me when an adoptable child was available.

Finally, after months and months of waiting, the attorney that we had hired in Port-Au-Prince called me and said, "Money talks in Haiti," and suggested that we bribe some government officials. I refused this option because, at the beginning of this adoption process, I asked my higher power to make this happen if it was the right thing or block it if it wasn't. So, we waited.

After a year of waiting, we got word of a little boy who had been abandoned at the gates of the orphanage. He was three years old, and as soon as the attorney was able to get a certificate of abandonment from the mayor, he could be adopted.

As it turned out, a physician friend of mine was in Haiti doing medical missions there. He agreed to see the boy. He reported that the boy was actually two years old, according to his evaluation, measured by his number of teeth, body build, and so on. He was a bit malnourished, had scabies, but was essentially well.

We adopted him while he was in Haiti and adopted him again after he got to the U.S. I did this to circumvent any problems. If the U.S. ever decided to get upset with the Haitian government or vice versa, everything would be settled. He was naturalized, and I'm so glad I'd had that forethought. We seem to not have a great relationship, currently or in history, with asylum seekers, especially from Haiti.

The sisters at the motherhouse did advise me not to spoil him because he seemed to have anger issues (like throwing himself on the floor and screaming) when he didn't get his way.

I was purposely strict as he grew up and mindful of telling him that he was loved, but he wasn't going to get by with misbehaving and tantrums. And he did get spanked on his bottom when he broke the rules.

He graduated high school and started college. College was not for him. He drank and did some drugs, as some kids do. He and his friend decided to join the Army one day without telling us. He announced it to us after the fact.

Over the years, he was deployed *four* times to the middle east: Afghanistan, Kabul, and Kuwait. He came back to us with full-blown mania, paranoia, PTSD, and was delusional, with bipolar type 1 and psychosis. He thought his friend was planning to chop him into pieces and freeze him and eat him over the winter. He thought we were stealing his "millions from those Gatorade and Nike contracts that he signed in High School track." He thought he was the "Black Jesus." There are so many more stories.

Why am I sharing this? So that people who have these and other issues regarding mental health know that they are not alone. There is always help. You are NOT your diagnosis.

After nine or ten years, my son's story is not yet over. We have twice had to admit him (involuntarily) for court-ordered treatment.

Presently, He lives in some veteran's apartments here in Phoenix and will allow no contact with us. Once every few

CHAPTER 9 | ALMOST HOME

months, I ask the Phoenix police to do a welfare check on him, just to make sure he is still alive. They are only allowed to give that much information because he is an adult and won't allow anything more.

I have four living children, and one who has moved on to the next place. There were certainly turbulent times and, later, estrangement. There were and still are separation and distrust from all directions. I haven't seen three of them for about 18-20 years, and we are missing each other's lives. I hate that. Mistakes were made by all of us. I vote for reconciliation at the earliest opportunity.

I will never give up on any of my children because they are not their diagnoses or their mistakes. They are very much loved. I hope to hear from them again. I hope to reunite with all of them, and maybe we can heal some of the brokenness. I hope that they will heal whatever is broken between themselves too. Time is short.

Part Two

At the beginning of this piece, I talked about my family history and explained some of the things that I've experienced and the wisdom I've gained along the way.

I'll start at the beginning.

My first memory was of being in a wooden crib with a clown holding three balloons in his glove, hand-painted on the headboard. He had sharp teeth. I was terrified of that clown being in my crib with me. I remember trying and trying to reach the top of the guardrails so I could pull myself out and run away. There was an empty double bed in that room. Someone slept in it sometimes, but there was nobody there now. Just a dark shadow that terrified me, and sometimes I thought it would come for me. I remember thinking in my terrified baby mind that if I wanted to keep from being crushed and destroyed, I would have to run.

There were times of abuse in my family, and there were some traumatic things that I don't recall at all. There are a lot of people in my life who have died, and I've managed to gain some wisdom from these experiences.

My mom died from kidney disease when I was six years old.

My grandfather shot himself in the head with a shotgun in my presence when I was six years old.

I have been the target of some familial sexual abuse.

My brother's son died from a gunshot to the chest.

I've had a cousin's son who died of a drug overdose.

I have had a cousin who was murdered on Christmas Day a few years ago.

I have an uncle who was killed many years ago. Three more uncles have passed and two aunts.

My dad died of a heart attack.

All my grandparents have passed.

Alcoholism runs rampant in the family

As I said, death is not a stranger to me. It's happened in my life all my life. I've often wondered, where did they go? Sometimes it feels like they are here, but I just cannot see them. Other times it feels so final and that they are silenced, or that I am silenced so they cannot hear me. I

CHAPTER 9 | ALMOST HOME

want them to hear me. I can see and hear them in my dreams, but that just makes me think that they're not far away. I do change my thinking on this subject from time to time.

In my life, I have been depressed and anxious with suicidal thoughts. I have been in therapy and medicated with antidepressants. Currently, I have a new antidepressant, and so far, it seems to be working well.

I've medicated with alcohol when I was unhappy in my marriage and in my job. I changed some things. Those things were helpful and hopeful. I've had sleep issues for as long as I can remember. They are improving.

I've had panic attacks and anxiety attacks. Panic is worse, very scary.

Here's the way Jenny Lawson describes it in her latest blog: "I've had anxiety attacks pretty regularly. Heart pounding, feelings of dread, some nausea. They don't last very long. Panic attacks are different. I only have one or two a year, but they are so severe it feels like I'm dying—like an actual heart attack. I've spent enough nights in the ER, sure I was dying, finding that this was a panic attack, but I didn't want to ruin Victor's birthday, so I explained it that it was too loud and went outside to get some air. I walked to the back of the restaurant and paced, trying in vain to walk away from what was inside me and doing all the meditation practices while cursing the fact that I'd stopped carrying Xanax with me. I suddenly felt incredibly nauseous and lightheaded, but I knew that if I started to throw up wouldn't be able to stop, so I sat down on the curb at the edge of the parking lot and put my head in between my knees and prayed Victor and Haley wouldn't come out because I didn't want them to see this. Then I heard footsteps, and I knew it was them, but it wasn't. It was a couple getting in their car nearby. The girl asked if I was okay, and I nodded yes, but she said I didn't look okay, which was fair, and I considered just saying I'd had too much to drink or that it was the flu, but instead, I said, "Panic attack," and she said "Oh yeah, he has them too!" and the guy was like, "The worst. Do you want us to sit with you or call someone, or do you need to be alone?"

"I said alone, because being with people makes it worse somehow, and they nodded. When they drove off, he said from their car window, "You got this, you're doing great." I was on the side of the road trying not to vomit, but somehow that small encouragement from a stranger helped. I mean, it didn't stop me from eventually getting violently sick, but it helped to know that I was not alone."

"Panic attacks are not normal, and I hate them. But I love that we've come so far that empathy for a person's struggle is normal, and we've come to a place where it's not a shameful secret but something that brings us together. It makes me hopeful." ~ Jenny Lawson, *thebloggess.com*.

I've absolutely felt like that in my life, and especially in this pandemic. Many of us have had our mental health issues exacerbated during this crazy time. Sometimes it is hard. I have learned that if you reach out, someone will be there to say, "Me too!" You are not your diagnosis. You are not what's happened to you. You are not what your inner critic is calling you. Stop the noise inside your head by talking with a trusted friend, someone who loves you

CHAPTER 9 | ALMOST HOME

without judgment. I do, and she knows who she is. We do it for each other.

Meditation helps me when I am sane enough to remember to do it.

Try to meditate by listening to the silence. Meditation was hard for me at first. I even had trouble remembering to do it at all. When I tried, my monkey mind could not stay clear for more than a few seconds, but with practice, the time lasted longer. I'm reminded to try every time I notice certain numbers lined up. A usual example is what I notice when I glance at the time. It might be 10:10 or 3:33, or 12:12. It reminds me to quiet the noise in my head, close my eyes and just pay attention to now. I even have my own little saying: stop, drop and listen. Stop (the noise) drop (my shoulders and tension in my body) and listen (for whatever comes), like a hummingbird or the scent of lemon blossoms in the breeze or the buzz of a bee nearby. Just plug into all that loveliness that is around and listen for the wisdom of right now. It's my meditation time, and it works for me and calms me and centers me in times of stress and distress.

I will be rewarded with being still and peaceful so that whatever comes is just what I need at that moment.

Maybe it's a sweet memory of my child, Ryan, who used to be here with us but is here no more. He was on this earth only 48 hours, but he is still in my heart all these 38 years later. It amazed me then and now, just thinking about how a soul in a body that tiny (two pounds, eight ounces) would go through all that is involved in the process of becoming—going through the birthing process—just to give me the wisdom that he did. I learned that being impatient hurts me, as well as others. I have learned not to quit before the miracle, as they say in AA. I learned a lot about loss. Losing a child is like losing an arm—you can try to replace it, but it's only a poor substitute and the pain and loss never really go away. There is an emptiness that I learned to keep in a special space in my heart. But I don't mind. To grieve is to know that I have a deep love for him.

Maybe it's a little pain from the past that we need to process until it's completely healed. Sometimes it's a large, crushing ache of which we have not yet discovered the source.

I only know that something will come when we listen. When our inner critic is not so loud and shrill.

There have been times, even recently, when I have forgotten to listen. It's an opportunity missed because that same lesson will keep showing up in my life until I get it, a little louder each time.

But I'm reminded to keep an open heart and mind, so even then, there is some wisdom to be learned.

My husband has quiet (and sometimes well hidden) little nuggets of wisdom that he shares at the time that he chooses. He has the patience of a saint, as they say, most of the time. But sometimes, when I'm loud and up in his face, he will blow—like a bad case of diarrhea. He rarely raises his voice, but he lets me know, with a raised eyebrow, that I've gone too far. Or said too much or crossed the crazy threshold.

CHAPTER 9 | ALMOST HOME

After two glasses of wine and a little chat with Jim, he said that we need to find something to do that's a fun way to spend retirement. His goal all his life was to make enough money to retire with enough income to really enjoy life and travel. He even likes to just ride around to see what's there. This is not the way I like to travel. I like to just get there already. Except when we're on our Harleys, then I like to ride around all day.

Recently, we took a trip to Huntington Beach, California. The traffic to get there was just horrendous. But we did get a hotel across the street, literally, from the Pacific Ocean. While there, we wanted to catch the ferry to Catalina Island to hang out there and eat lunch. Due to Covid-19, we were unable to get on the ferry because they were booked as full as they could be with social distancing.

We attempted to get on different boat cruises, but due to the damn Covid-19 virus, they were fully booked throughout the week. Every day, we would go out to eat, order twice as much as we needed so we could feed the same homeless people that we saw every day. We walked around till our legs hurt and never really saw much besides the pier and the surrounding five or six blocks.

But it was lovely to get away from the Arizona heat, and we did gain some wisdom from all the homeless. Many were mentally ill and talking to and sometimes arguing with people that nobody else saw. But they knew that at that moment, they were seen and heard. Many had interesting stories, and others were clearly not present. They are not their illness, and while we were there, they were not alone. It was good for us to be reminded just how privileged we are. For a moment, we got to remember and practice what Ram Dass taught, "We're all just walking each other home."

Chapter Ten

Flying Through Fear: How to Change Everything
By Donna Kiel

Donna Kiel

Donna Kiel is a life coach, energy healer, teacher, leader, university professor, and a guide for those seeking their best life. Donna has a unique ability to inspire you to discover and live your highest potential. Donna's expertise, training, and engaging and welcoming style provide the compassion and connection needed to discover your own genius and passion. Donna is a coach, mentor, best-selling author, professor, and architect of change who works for equity and empathy in every context. Donna holds a doctorate in educational leadership and is a certified counselor and trained life coach. Donna created the empathy framework with practical tools to lead individuals and organizations to experience new levels of connection, creativity, and success.

Donna is often sought for innovative change efforts by organizations and individuals seeking solutions to systemic and life challenges. Donna inspires, enlivens, and creates useful and practical solutions. Donna is the epitome of inspiration and integrity for those seeking meaning, insight, and concrete answers to the next steps in life. Donna is currently a professor, speaker, coach, and mentor offering workshops, individual coaching, anxiety relief, career planning, and life mapping sessions.

She can be reached at drdonnakiel@gmail.com or through her website at https://donnakiel.com.

Flying Through Fear: How to Change Everything

By Donna Kiel

What are you afraid of? What is at the core of that fear? Pain? Death? Failure? Not being worthy? Explore that, and then ask yourself what you would be without that fear. These questions came to me as a text. As I read the words, I wondered how this had all happened. The text was from Dr. Jill Bolte Taylor.

Dr. Taylor is the Harvard-trained neuroanatomist who is the author of the New York Times best-selling book, *My Stroke of Insight*, and who has the most-watched TED Talk of all time by the same title. If you haven't watched that TED Talk, stop right now and watch it. How was it that Dr. Jill Bolte Taylor was reaching out to me with her expertise and her wisdom to guide me through some of the worst fear of my life? It all seemed rather surreal. Then again, my life for the last year had been surreal. This segment of my life has given me a pathway to authentic wisdom that surpassed anything I knew in my previous 61 years. That wisdom has given me the power to change everything and spread my wings to fly through fear to freedom. I want to give you the same.

Let me take you on my journey of meeting Dr. Taylor and the discovery of the wisdom that transformed my life. Let's start with a bit of background on me. From outward cultural norms, I am a highly successful woman with a

CHAPTER 10 | FLYING THROUGH FEAR: HOW TO CHANGE EVERYTHING

doctorate in education and a dream job as a faculty member at a prominent university. I am surrounded by incredible friends and family who are loving, kind, supportive, funny, and imperfectly wonderful. From outward appearances, you might conclude I was a confident, calm, and engaging person who navigated life with ease. It sure does look that way. However, that's not the truth. The truth is that I am a person who wakes each morning in a state of panic and fear about almost everything. I am a highly introverted and uncertain woman of deep empathy. Much of my success came from a quest to prove I was worth being on the planet by overachieving and people-pleasing

When the pandemic hit, my fear kicked into overdrive. I was consumed with fear I would lose my faculty position and the life coaching and workshops I did on the side. Without those titles and affirmation, how would my life matter? My solution was to kick up the gear on my typical ten-hour workdays to become sixteen-hour workdays that were filled with helping everyone I could think of to deal with the challenges of the pandemic. When I was consumed with helping others, I was distracted from my fears and worries. Six months into the pandemic, I noticed my hair was shedding more than usual. A virtual meeting with my doctor led to blood tests and a mammogram. As I shared my work schedule with my doctor, her response was frightening. She strongly said that I needed to cut back and stop working so hard. A new fear was entering my anxiety-ridden mind—that of fear of my mortality.

For the next four months, I carried on reducing work a bit, though not much. Then, in a Zoom meeting in which I was leading a workshop for school principals, one of the principals seemed to have had dental surgery. Her mouth was frozen on one side. As we were doing discussions, the principal revealed she had been stricken with Bell's palsy. Her entire face was paralyzed on one side. My body had a strange reaction. Just a couple of weeks before this Zoom workshop, while wearing my mask, I had noticed what I thought was drool in the corner of my mouth. During the Zoom meeting, fear rushed through my body. Was I getting Bell's palsy too? My gut had told me something was wrong. Yet, I didn't interrupt work to check it out.

As the vaccination emerged and the world began to open up, I had a new fear. I had come to enjoy working long hours in the safety of my home. Now everyone was eager to get back to in-person meetings and connect. My introversion had become far more intense during the pandemic. I didn't want to go back to being around people. I was safer and had this illusion of control in the safety of my home. It was a question from my closest friend about going on vacation together that pushed me over the edge. Rather than answer whether I wanted to get away, I shouted, "I need to get to the doctor about this sensation in my lip that is not going away!" I shocked her and myself.

During a virtual visit with the doctor, she asked me to puff out my cheeks and then to pucker my lips. Her requests to me made my heart pound harder, and fear swelled up in my throat. Something was wrong, and I could see it on her face. I could feel a small bump just in front of my ear. It was something—but what was it? The doctor ordered a CT scan and blood work. She told me to call if anything changed or grew worse.

CHAPTER 10 | FLYING THROUGH FEAR: HOW TO CHANGE EVERYTHING

The next day, during a Zoom meeting, I thought my lip was now feeling numb. I called the doctor. She said I should go to the emergency room. The CT scan and MRI revealed a tumor on my salivary gland. The emergency room doctors said I'd need to see a surgeon to have a biopsy and have it removed.

It is amazing how your world can shift in just a moment. My son went with me to the surgeon. The professor in me took charge. I went into the meeting with the agenda that I would get scheduled for surgery, have this thing removed, and get back to work. My agenda would be trashed in the first five minutes of the meeting. The surgeon began to explain the complexity of this surgery and how difficult it would be to save my facial nerve. I felt sick to my stomach. My son's wedding was in three months. The surgeon said I should wait until after the wedding that the wait was not a risk. So, for the next three months, I interviewed surgeons to find the best one. I researched, prayed, worried, and fretted over the surgery. It was torturous and the most intense journey inward that I could imagine.

During the three long months as I waited for surgery, I wrote to God each day. I wrote of my fear, my hopes, my prayers for surgery to be a success. I prayed for the biopsy to be benign and to choose the right surgeon. I created a ritual of writing to God, then meditating, connecting with God, and then allowing God to speak through a letter to me. The letters from God were filled with love, acceptance, and guidance to start living with eyes of love. The letters continually told me that I had all I needed to get through the uncertainty and the unknown. In my letters to God, I begged forgiveness from those I had harmed and vowed to forgive those who had hurt me. I worked on myself through energy healing and deep exploration of the source of all these fears. I discovered that so many of my fears were stories I created in my mind rather than fears of true impending harm.

Perhaps the most important discovery during this long period of waiting and worry was the true fragility of life and the importance of valuing each moment. My son's wedding was a moment of awe and joy beyond anything I had ever experienced. Before his wedding, I engaged in events with the emotional desire to just get through it so I could be alone again. I dismissed my angst in social situations by waving my introversion flag. I would always be the one at an event checking my phone and needing to get back to work as I had important things to do. Even as I was with my own family, I would be distracted from connecting by working or worrying about work. I had been avoiding the rich emotional complexity of life by claiming roles and responsibilities that were also denying me the joy of life.

My son's wedding was different. My long journey inward had shown me the true priority of just connecting and being within the present moment. For the first time, I wasn't rushing to please someone or do something. I didn't focus on how I would appear or look – I just was present and filled with love and joy. Yet, in the back of my mind was that once the wedding was over, I would have just two weeks until this complicated surgery.

The pre-surgery prognosis was that my face would need at least three months to a year to fully recover so that I had

CHAPTER 10 | FLYING THROUGH FEAR: HOW TO CHANGE EVERYTHING

full movement. I had prayed each day for a quick recovery – immediate recovery of my smile and movement. The surgery lasted nine hours. As I woke from surgery, my daughter was by my side. She was talking about work and getting me some dinner. The nurses were saying, "Look, she can close her eye." I could speak, but my mouth felt dry. I wanted to know if everything was alright.

Though I had three months to imagine the impact of the surgery—all those images could never predict the drains in my neck, the feeling of not being able to smile fully, and having a hard time eating. I had been someone who was never tired and could do anything. Now, just drinking water was a struggle. The resident told me that there was one tumor with several little nodules around it. The day after surgery, the surgeon came to release me. He said he would see me the next week in his office to discuss follow-up.

After being at home anxiously musing about what was next, I had enough. It was my 62nd birthday, and I needed to take charge of my life. I had watched a webinar with Dr. Jill Bolte Taylor about her new book, *Whole Brain Living*. I hung on every word as she described the anatomy of our brain and how knowing this anatomy and understanding the two hemispheres and how they work could give us the choice of how we experience life. Her words that whole-brain living is a "road map to peace, which really is just a thought away" were like a balm to my soul. I had tried Dr. Taylor's 90-second rule to manage my anxiety. The 90-second rule is the neuroscientific reality that any emotional circuit of feelings, whether anxiety, fear or sorrow, will run its course and stop after the 90 seconds that it takes for the chemistry to neutralize. It is the cell anatomy of the way our neurons fire. If we can eliminate the retriggering of the circuit, we can know that the challenging emotion will be done in 90 seconds. Dr. Taylor's work had truly shifted my thinking.

Before the surgery, I had watched Dr. Taylor do a live online meeting with Martha Beck, the New York Times best-selling author who created the life coaching program I completed. Two of my true heroes of wisdom were together talking about healing. Martha had had surgery on her foot, and Dr. Taylor had given her guidance as to how to heal more quickly by using her brain's power to rewire the circuitry.

And so, on my birthday, after enduring three months of relentless anxiety and having to face the physical limitations of surgery, I decided to reach out to Jill Bolte Taylor. First, I thought about asking the Martha Beck team how I could reach Dr. Taylor. I quickly decided no to that idea. I wanted to do this on my own. I wanted to use Dr. Taylor's work in my research, and I wanted her guidance and advice on healing. I wanted to shift my life and create my path of meaning and impact. For most of my life, I had worked for the agenda of everyone else. I was facing the unknown reality of my mortality, and I wanted to take charge of my life, my destiny, and my purpose.

I went to Dr. Taylor's website and found the "contact us" portion. I filled out the form with who I was and what I wanted. On the afternoon of my 62nd birthday, I clicked send and figured that would be it. I didn't imagine that I would hear from anyone for a long time, but I felt I had done something—not sure what—but I had asked if I could

CHAPTER 10 | FLYING THROUGH FEAR: HOW TO CHANGE EVERYTHING

research the impact of Dr. Taylor's work on others and if I could ask her guidance on how to heal my face. I put it out there.

That evening while my family ate pizza and celebrated my birthday, I scrolled through on my phone to pass the time. I saw an email from "Jill" and wondered who that was. Reading the email felt surreal. It was simple. "Let's meet. I'm pretty full this week, but perhaps we can meet in the evening." I quickly replied, "I'm happy to meet anytime that fits your schedule." I wondered who I was emailing. Was this an assistant, a bot, or a scam? Within a few minutes, there was a reply. "Let's meet tomorrow at 8:00 p.m. Can you send a Zoom?" I kept reading it—was this real?

Without fear or hesitation, I sent a Zoom link to meet with Dr. Jill Bolte Taylor. I had a drain in my neck, could barely move my mouth to talk, and looked like hell. For the first time in my life, it didn't matter. I wanted to take care of myself, to do work that I wanted to do, and to have a meaningful impact.

Over the next few weeks, Dr. Taylor and I talked and explored whole brain living, my researching her work, my post-surgical prognosis, and the recommendation that even though all things were benign, I should do radiation. Jill shared with me her journey and talked me through my brain's four characters and how they were being revealed in my anxiety as well as my creativity. She gave me her neuroanatomical expertise on radiation and proton radiation.

I came to deeply understand the neuroscience that defines our brain and how it all works. I had read Dr. Taylor's book, *Whole Brain Living*, a few times over, but hearing her speak and walk me through whole brain living was transformational. We chatted several times about how I could research the impact of her method on school communities. She introduced me to her amazing colleagues. At times I thought I was dreaming or that pain meds had me in a very wild dream state. As we talked about research, we also talked about our lives. I shared my fears about the radiation, and that the doctors all directed me to a path I didn't want. I found myself not only in awe of Dr. Taylor, but quickly growing in authentic appreciation and fondness of Jill.

Each day, as I confronted my sorrow and anxiety, I applied Dr. Taylor's "BRAIN huddle" exercise from *Whole Brain Living*. Simply put, we have two hemispheres in our brain—right and left. Each hemisphere has both an emotional brain and a thinking brain. So, there are four modules to our brain. Dr. Taylor has truly provided us with a clear, concise roadmap for understanding the two hemispheres and the four distinct modules of cells as four characters that make up who we are: Character 1—left thinking; Character 2—left emotion; Character 3—right emotion; and Character 4—right thinking. In the BRAIN huddle, we breathe, recognize, appreciate, inquire, and navigate our way to our own choice of how we live our lives.

In whole brain living, we learn the neuroscience and psychology that everything we think, feel, or do is dependent upon brain cells to perform that function. The

CHAPTER 10 | FLYING THROUGH FEAR: HOW TO CHANGE EVERYTHING

four modules, which Jill calls characters, form specific groups of cells that feel unique inside of our bodies. Each of our four characters displays particular skills, feels specific emotions, and thinks distinctive thoughts.

I got to know my four characters more deeply in chats with Jill. My Character 1 is that part of me that was a highly successful school principal and professor who loved to organize research and create compelling projects. My Character 2, which dominated my life, was that part of me that held the trauma of a little girl who had been sexually molested and who always feared her parents would abandon her. My Character 2 was filled with the shame of being bullied as a fat little kid and whose introversion made social settings painful. My Character 3 is the playful and open-hearted side of me who climbs on a camel and plays pretend with my two-year-old granddaughter. And then there is my cherished Character 4, who is that part of me that feels God in moments of hardship and bliss, who forgives instantly and loves unconditionally.

Knowing that our brains are these wonderfully rich sources of the order, organization, and structure of Character 1, the trauma-holding of Character 2, the playfulness and creativity of Character 3, and the God-moments of grace of Character 4, can change everything in your life. If you know these four characters, you can choose which one is in charge. For me, it is my Character 4 that gives me the wings from which to fly through fear and into freedom.

Changing anything in your life is completely within reach as you apply the 90-second rule, love and appreciate all four characters and let who you want to take charge. What is your fear telling you? Who would you be without that fear? Having wisdom is knowing that life is a deliciously sad, fearful, joyful, peaceful, and loving place. Feel it all and fly free!

Chapter Eleven

When Opportunity Knocks, Open The Door
By Amy I. King

Amy I. King

Amy I. King is a certified life coach and owner of Your Phenomenal Life, LLC. She taught in public education for a decade before returning to school for her coaching certification. She is a contributing author of the international best sellers: *Inspirations: 101 Uplifting Stories for Daily Happiness*, *Manifestations: True Stories of Bringing the Imagined into Reality*, and *The Grateful Soul: The Art and Practice of Gratitude*, among others.

Amy enjoys spending time with friends, listening to great music of a variety of genres, reading, writing, and adventure. She enjoys traveling—both solo and with loved ones— and she loves meeting new people and making new connections.

Amy has overcome a plethora of challenges that make her the woman she is today. She was born with spina bifida, which now requires her to use a wheelchair. Despite the many challenges she has faced, she has created a life that is filled with wonderful people who have helped her create amazing memories. She has most recently overcome breast cancer. Every challenge, Amy believes, is put before us to help us to evolve and grow into the greatest version of ourselves.

Amy's greatest joy is using her personal experiences and wisdom to help others move past their personal blocks and outdated beliefs to become empowered to live the life of their dreams.

She loves developing relationships with her clients built on trust and vulnerability. She is currently coaching, taking improv classes, and working on her first solo book, *Messy Wheels: Stories from Where I Sit*, available on Amazon in 2022. She can be reached at (916) 718-0914. She welcomes the opportunity to work with you to help you build the life of your dreams.

When Opportunity Knocks, Open the Door

By Amy I. King

As we flew over the Sahara Desert, my eyes peering through the oval window next to my seat, exhausted tears began to well up. I wrote in my journal, "I have seen the breathtaking view of the Sahara Desert! So overwhelming and beautiful in its unique way."

A few months earlier, on a beautiful spring Sunday after church, we sat at the dining room table of my pastor, breaking bread. It was not often that I was anywhere else on a Sunday afternoon at that time in my life. My pastor had unofficially adopted me into his large beautiful family. Eight grandchildren played dolls and basketball or sat around on the two couches watching football games or helping out in the kitchen with the adults. It felt amazing to belong to something so filled with love.

My pastor's son-in-law, who himself is a pastor and originally from Nigeria, stated, "We are planning a mission trip to Africa to start building a medical clinic in the village of Aklampa, The Republic of Benin and also to visit my home in Lagos, Nigeria." I could feel the excitement building inside of me.

While in college, I had taken four classes in African history and the African diaspora as part of my history degree. I was elated to finally have the opportunity to visit a continent that I had studied but only dreamed I could see! I took a sip

CHAPTER 11 | WHEN OPPORTUNITY KNOCKS, OPEN THE DOOR

of punch from my cup as I heard my inner voice say, "This is the opportunity that you have been waiting for; you have to go!" I was in from the first mention.

A few months prior to the opportunity being presented, I graduated from college. my mother had gifted me a certificate good for a plane ticket to "anywhere in the world." Travel was imperative to my mom. She knew the value and education that travel to foreign countries provided. She instilled a sense of wonder and adventure about the world, and I could not be more grateful. The more I saw of this world, the more I wanted to see. So, this was how I was going to use the ticket. I was going to not one, but two countries in Africa!

I was employed at the time in the computer software industry as a quality assurance tester. So, I had a decision to make, do I stay, or do I go? Of course, I was a temp, so my job wouldn't be held. But, it was a pretty straightforward decision that I was willing to risk the job for the sake of fulfilling a dream. So, I gave my two weeks' notice and packed my luggage.

There were seventeen people in the group that I was traveling with who met for several weeks beforehand. We learned a few French phrases to get by, we learned about culture and manners, what we would need to do to prepare for the trip, things to purchase, vaccinations required, and so on. And we got to know each other a little bit.

I went to the airport in early October, where I waited with several others from our group. It would be a twenty-three-hour journey to Africa with a total of three legs to our trip. With nervous anticipation, we boarded the first plane taking us to Ohio. Then it was off to Brussels, Belgium, with another layover. On that leg, I met two men who were traveling together. One of the men was from Belgium, the other, Holland. Finally, we boarded the plane that would take us to the Republic of Benin with a brief stop to let passengers disembark and board in Ivory Coast. A few men struck conversations with me, curious about where I came from. As we exited the plane, I felt the sticky heat of the evening hit me. I was born with spina bifida and, at the time, used forearm crutches and had AFOs (ankle-foot orthotics) on both legs. I painstakingly went backward down each step from the airplane, on my crutches.

It had been so many hours since I had slept. Too amped up for sleep on the plane, exhaustion was setting in. About twenty-five men met us at the airport, which, almost 25 years ago, resembled a roof with supports. We were given the VIP treatment because one of the men meeting us was a high-ranking military official; we went through customs without having our bags checked. A couple of women and I got into an Isuzu Trooper with a man who spoke no English. One of the women accidentally dropped a notebook behind her. We heard a chicken clucking, and then it stopped. The ride took about 30 minutes. As we drove, I peered out the window at shanties (three-sided stands) of corrugated metal and scrap wood that doubled as storefronts and homes approximately ten feet by five feet, illuminated by flame. Finally, we reached the hotel where we would be staying for the first few nights while our visas were straightened out, as the embassy was giving the group trouble. I took a shower and joined the rest of the group for dinner, consisting of a whole fish, rice, a potato salad, and tomato followed by lemon pound cake. It was delicious and

CHAPTER 11 | WHEN OPPORTUNITY KNOCKS, OPEN THE DOOR

filled my stomach. I went back to my room, where I fell into bed and slept the entire night.

The following day, I woke refreshed. We headed to Ganvie (gon-vi-ay), a floating city established in 1717 about eight kilometers off the land. It is a community of 25,000 people who live in homes that are built on stilts. They get to them by canoe. There is a school, church, shops, and even a hotel. Our guide moved the boat by plunging a long stick of wood into the water. He would hit the bottom of the river on which the city was built and push us forward, wearing his traditional dashiki in a beautiful orange and blue pattern and black sunglasses. He pulled up alongside one of the shops, and we were let off. I had to be very careful not to stick a crutch between the planks laid on the floor, as it could break, and my mobility would be impacted. I learned that lesson when I was in Japan. Inside the store, there were numerous souvenirs; my eyes went to a painting on canvas tacked to the wall. The image, titled Co-existence, had a warm blue background; it features three people dressed in robes sitting around a table enjoying coffee and each other's company. I asked, "how much," the man told me the equivalent of $50, one of the chaperones said, too much. He came back again with a lower number, and I said okay. My chaperone told me that I still paid too much. Twenty dollars seemed like a bargain to me. It hangs on my kitchen wall today as a reminder of an incredible adventure.

The next day, we went to the Topay open market. We exited the vans and were overwhelmed with the bright colors, various sounds, and scents of delicious foods, almost anything you can think of wanting or needing. Food, clothes, souvenirs, and household items were available for purchase. There were rows and rows of vendors selling their goods. A group of children followed me around, trying to sell me whatever they had in their possession. My bodyguard got into conversation with a man. I asked what he was saying. He told me that he was offered dowry for me and that he was trying to negotiate. Hilarious! The smog was noxious in the market area as emissions aren't under strict regulations. After the market, we were invited by some people who work at the American embassy to attend a church service. Afterward, we were invited to their home for dinner.

The following day we were supposed to travel to the village of Aklampa to break ground, but we were delayed another day.

The next day, we went to the Nigerian Embassy, followed by the American Embassy. Our visas were granted, and we were off to the village. The journey was supposed to take four hours, but it took eleven hours to get to the village where we would be laying the first brick of the medical clinic that was being built. Before having the clinic, the village residents had to walk for days to receive medical attention. The last few miles of our journey were down a muddy road. The vans kept getting stuck, forcing the men to get out and push. Finally, when we got close enough, we could hear music in the distant darkness. The village residents had been celebrating all day in honor of our arrival with song and dance for us! Happy tears formed and began to fall.

We finally arrived and quickly gathered on the porch of the home where we would be staying. People were singing and dancing and performing for us! A young boy (the nephew

CHAPTER 11 | WHEN OPPORTUNITY KNOCKS, OPEN THE DOOR

of the pastor) approached me. Eventually, he ended up on my lap, and we were all but inseparable for the duration of our stay in the village. He has the most beautiful eyes of anyone I have ever seen in my entire life. If you saw them, you would understand. He has since passed them down to his son. After about three hours, we went to our respective dwellings, took cup baths (a bucket of water and a cup), and went to bed. The bedroom was a double bed that I shared with another woman. There was an area in the bedroom with a drain on the floor for bathing. The toilet was outside in the outhouse built especially for us. The windows had no glass, only wood slats that opened and closed. We lived with a bat who would fly in at night. Although there was no electricity, we had a generator that would provide energy to the one light in the common area. We used lanterns, too.

The following day I woke to a young man sweeping my room. I got up, bathed, and sat on the porch where many of the children had gathered. Some of the children touched my wet ponytail with curiosity.

Our group visited the home of the pastor's mother. She was so sweet! Later that day, the King of the village greeted us, one by one, at his palace, where we were treated to a performance by stilt walkers, singers, and dancers. I later learned that he was amazed that someone with a disability would travel to another country to help.

Our visit to the elementary school to give children the gifts that we had brought was enjoyable. All of the children were dressed in their uniforms. They were standing in the straightest lines, by grade level. All the children were thrilled to receive the little candies and gumball machine-type gifts. We visited their classrooms and talked with the students. I took a walk with the doctor who had come with us. We walked around the village in conversation while goats and chickens roamed around haphazardly. I noticed a bar among the dwellings. It was a tiny place with a long table and plastic chairs to stop in for a libation.

When we turned a corner, we kept walking and came upon the beautiful scene of a multigenerational family. Mom cooking in front of their home, the men off to the side, playing mancala, a young girl with a baby strapped to her back, and three little boys joyously playing with sticks and definitely in a land of make-believe. The challenges that all of the people in the village faced were not evident on their faces.

Two of the guys from our group and I took a walk the following day and ended up at the bar for a quick and secret beer. The bar was literally a long table and chairs. The bartender was a woman who would leave the dwelling from the back and return with beer and three small glasses. It's a unique experience to enjoy a beer in a bar in a remote village in Africa and one of my fondest memories.

Our final day in the village included a celebration in our honor in the afternoon. That evening we were at the house having dinner when one of the women mistakenly sipped from a water bottle used for kerosene. The doctor quickly administered medication, but the retching and coughing were awful! She was in a lot of pain.

That night, the doctor and I sat on the porch. We talked and held hands. I was sad to be leaving. The singer in the village came by and gave me a gift. A small hand-carved

CHAPTER 11 | WHEN OPPORTUNITY KNOCKS, OPEN THE DOOR

wood elephant that I display in my home. The doctor kissed me goodnight. I was taken aback.

The following day at 7:30 a.m., we were headed back to Cotonou and then on to Lagos. We stopped for lunch at 12:30 at a restaurant because the vans were having issues and we were behind schedule. One had a cracked gas line, the other a hole in the exhaust. We returned to Cotonou at 4:30 p.m. and decided to go on to Nigeria. We reached the Nigerian border at 7:00 p.m. and were detained by military police with machine guns until midnight. The corruption was evident. They were making us bribe them to get across the border. We ended up at a hotel near the country's border because it wasn't safe to drive to Lagos that late at night. We would move to the Bible Guest House, a hostel with single rooms, in the morning.

We had lunch and then went to the outdoor market. On the way back to the hostel, there was bumper-to-bumper traffic. People were selling everything and anything on the side of the road. They would come to the cars with their goods. One of the guys bought a loaf of bread.

The next day we visited one of the clinics supported by the foundation that we were representing. I then was able to see the home of the pastor's mom. The following day, three of the women from our group and I ventured to Porto Novo in a taxi driven by a lovely man named Dossou. We stopped at a restaurant for refreshments and then went to two museums, one of which was the former palace of the King.

I remember thinking I'm going to Africa to help others. The reality was that it was an opportunity for me to expand by seeing life through someone else's lens. I feel that I gained more than I could have ever given. I returned with a greater understanding of the world around me, my place in it, and my duty to make it a better place for everyone. The knowledge that we are all the same was reinforced in me. I learned that people are happier when they are in cooperation as opposed to competition. I was raised to be competitive, but a tiny part of that died in Africa. My entire perspective shifted. I came home and felt that I had too much. I began conserving water when I showered, choosing Navy showers (if you know, you know) over free-flowing long luxurious ones.

When an opportunity presents itself, it is our responsibility to say yes to what resonates. Opportunities do not often present themselves more than once, and you never know what lies around the corner. Less than a year after that trip, I began having trouble with my gait. It was becoming more and more challenging to use crutches. I eventually became a full-time wheelchair user. A wheelchair would have made the trip to Africa much more complex, and parts would have been impossible. When you feel something deep inside of you speak, listen. Grab the opportunities that life presents you. The only regrets we should ever have are about what we have done, not things we wish we had done. You never know what life is going to hand you. Life is happening now. Do what makes you happy and when opportunity knocks, answer the door.

Chapter Twelve

Being Beautifully Boxed
By Paula Meyer

Paula Meyer

After becoming a widow at 54, Paula Meyer left her job and began a year of travel to heal her heart. As her travel ended, the Covid-19 pandemic began. The strategies for navigating the grief of her husband's death from throat cancer also helped with the grief from the pandemic and social unrest.

Losing her freedom and lifestyle, she was thrown into the unknown just as her new business began. Her new book, *Great Loss, Greater Love: The Art & Heart of Navigating Grief*, chronicles her year of travel and is a #1 International Bestseller on Amazon.

Paula has 30+ years of experience as an event planner and contracting specialist, with 12 years in author/speaker management. She has organized and managed 151 workshops around the world. Her company, GP Eventworx, specializes in event production for speaker/teacher workshops, as well as grief retreats for women.

She has traveled to 20 countries, some multiple times, and 42 U.S. states. Her goal is to visit 30 countries and all 56 U.S. states and territories by the end of 2025. Learn more at www.greatlossgreaterlove.com

Being Beautifully Boxed
By Paula Meyer

How many times have you heard the phrase, "get out of the box?" When you hear that phrase directed at you, does it make you squirm? Does it make you angry? Does fear bubble up? Or do you feel joy and freedom? Does it make you want to expand or contract? And does it entice you to take a leap into the unknown?

Now take a minute to think about your answers to these questions. Take the time to list out a few bullet points for each one, just one or two words that explain the feelings that arose. Then ask yourself, or more pointedly ask spirit, why do these words represent that feeling, and what do they really mean for you?

I've found that if you can determine the "why" and the "meaning" of the fearful ones, you'll get closer to creating a way to move the lower energy out and create space to bring higher energy in.

Now think about your box, which is really your energetic comfort zone. It's the very real, but mostly unseen, protective walls and boundaries that you've created throughout your life that you are currently living in.

There's nothing wrong with your current box, as it can be many things, from our sacred space for self-care to a private place for protection and comfort. It can also be our dream and planning spot, our creation station.

CHAPTER 12 | BEING BEAUTIFULLY BOXED

What does your box look like? Is it just four solid walls made of brick, wood, or cement, with a short flat ceiling? Maybe you've increased your square footage by configuring it with six or even eight sides. You may have changed the roof line to accommodate vaulted ceilings to feel more expansive.

Are there any windows or skylights? Where are they placed? Is natural light streaming in? Are the windows covered? Are they open, allowing fresh air to blow in? Is the glass clear or frosted? Windows allow you to see outside your box, to dream and see possibility.

I believe we have a few versions of the box that we live in at any given moment, depending on what's happening in our lives. Let's take a tour through these boxes.

Depriver Box

This is a four-sided cube, where every wall is the same size. There is a front door facing north representing the future, which is firmly shut and locked. There is a small window, covered up, where you sometimes peek through at the horrific possibilities and confirm that nothing good is in your future. On the south wall, there is a back door representing the past, which is wide open with wind and rain constantly blowing in. There is no need for a window as you can plainly see everything through the open door. The sights and sounds are scary and hard to close off. On the east and west walls, there are tiny windows that are closed tight and covered up. The ceiling is low and flat. There is a door outside of the house leading into the basement, but you don't even know it's there. In this box, there is no forward movement and no sitting still in the moment. All that scares you about the future pulls you back ever further into the past. It's all about backward movement while frantically scraping and clawing to not get pulled out the back door. The serious pendulum swing between the front and back doors is exhausting. Outside your box is a very high wall that not only keeps people out but it keeps you in.

Survivor Box

This box has the same configuration as the depriver box, with the following improvements: The front door has a small window at the top to allow light in. The window next to the door is partially covered but still closed, as are the small east and west windows. The back door is still open, but it has a screen door so that at least nothing gets blown in. And the ceiling is still low and flat. In this box, you are not moving forward, but thankfully you have slowed down the backward movement. At least enough to cancel out the scary forward movement so that you tread water and stay in place. It's still exhausting, but most of your energy is used to remain neutral. And this neutral space is not about being in the present moment. The pendulum isn't swinging so much anymore. It's just a zero-sum game. No one wins a game like that. But at least you sometimes allow yourself to peek out the windows. This peeking out is what moves you to the next version. And you get a glimpse of that door outside, which leads to the basement. Sometimes you go out the front and back doors, but you do this as quickly as possible for tasks that need to be done outside of your box,

CHAPTER 12 | BEING BEAUTIFULLY BOXED

like a job or family responsibilities. You very rarely look at or try to understand what's outside of either door. All you can see when you look out is that tall fence that surrounds your box.

Revivor Box

This box has the same configuration as the depriver and survivor boxes, yet it's starting to revive and expand! The ceiling is no longer flat but is now angled to a high point in the center, with a small skylight on the north side, revealing a beautiful sunny blue sky by day and the North Star by night. The front door is now open with a screen door, allowing light and fresh air to come in. The front window is twice as big, and it's open. The east and west windows are bigger too. And the back door is now a French door, overlooking a beautiful garden. A door is a level up from a window. A door allows you to see out and gives you a choice to take that step out after having daydreamed at the window. You can now step out and experience your daydream, experience your desires, feel outside of your box. You are now inspired to walk out the front and back door and spend some time outside looking at things. You are not as fearful as you become aware of what's around your box. As you venture out the back door, you finally approach the door leading into the basement, and you are pleasantly surprised. This represents your inner self, your spirit, the true you, and you eagerly open the door and peek in. It's a bit dark, only because you haven't adjusted your eyes yet. You feel the good vibes that are there, and you are intrigued to connect. When you open that door, you feel the tingling in your heart, and you know that you want to get closer. As you emerge from the sacred doorway, you see that the wall around your box is much shorter now, and you can see through it to what's on the other side.

Thriver Box

As the tingling in your heart increases, your awareness of who you really are begins to become clearer. As clarity increases, the door to your heart opens and allows all the doors and windows in your box to open. You are beginning to understand being in the present moment, and this confidence allows you to investigate both your future and your past and see possibilities before you! You become aware of the gifts and lessons of your past, how they created who you are now, and how that can shape and create an amazing new future! You realize all the good and bad experiences have something in common; they were experiences to help you create the life you do want. Suddenly your box now has eight sides to it, with windows on every wall. Then you notice that every wall has a beautiful French doorway so that you can easily walk through to experience something new! Each window and door reveal unlimited possibilities each time you look through the window and open the door! As your energy is uplifted by the new experiences, the windows and doors open to higher experiences that will take you even farther!

The ceiling is now a soaring, vaulted ceiling with skylights on each panel, allowing the light and energy of spirit to be infused down into your haven. The outside is a beautiful garden surrounding your box, filled with your favorite

CHAPTER 12 | BEING BEAUTIFULLY BOXED

flowers and trees. You may have an abundant vegetable garden or an overflowing orchard of many varieties of fruits. The enclosure wall has now become a short and beautifully crafted wrought iron fence that allows you to see and be seen. And the basement door is always open, allowing you to go inward and connect to your spirit so that you are thriving on every level! If you have a challenging day, that inner stairwell to spirit is always there to support and uplift you. You are no longer afraid of your power, and the darkness that was once in the stairwell is now beautifully lit all along the way. In this new house, you are never alone and always loved and supported.

Many times, I find myself in the depriver, survivor, or revivor boxes. The more time I spend in my thriver box, I root that memory into my being, which allows me to remember I don't have to stay in those lower boxes. Once you become more aware of the thriver box and spend quality time there, you can more quickly and easily get back there. There is no need to abandon your box, just love into it and level it up to match your new energy. There may be things in your box that you need to let go of when the time is right. Let go with love and gratitude, and then fill the space with more love. There is always more love, never-ending love.

The wisdom is in the journey. As you move through and forward, and occasionally backward, you re-imagine and transform your box. You find that it's not about being boxed in, then. It's about creating your sacred haven where you rest, rejuvenate, imagine, re-imagine, and create ever anew! You gain more wisdom, and these golden nuggets and pearls build up your resiliency. They remind you of your innate power to create a life of beauty. They show you that you are so much more than just a human body in a box. When you open and expand your box, you encourage your body to open and expand, and then spirit can shine through you in all its wonder-filled majesty!

Chapter Thirteen

Stepping Into the Crone Wisdom
By Maggie Morris

Maggie Morris

Maggie is an authentic, caring, sensitive soul with a passion for nurturing others with her soul love. Maggie lives her gifts of service to humanity through her generosity and her ability to ignite the flame in others to see their limitless possibilities. Maggie uses her intuition and connection with spirit to be an example of strength and courage to all she meets. Now, as an author, public speaker, life coach, mindfulness master/mentor, meditation facilitator, and death doula, Maggie continues to pursue her passions as well as helping those she connects with to find healing. Maggie loves and lives to encourage others to passionately become their authentic self by choosing healing through letting go of limiting beliefs that hold you back.

You can reach Maggie through her website at www.whispersofwisdom.ca or through Facebook.

Stepping Into the Crone Wisdom
By Maggie Morris

It's quite surreal beginning to write for *Wisdom Keepers* in the very same week that my first grandchild takes his place in the family. I have now become the one carrying the wisdom of the grandmother.

In all my years of life and in all the wisdom I have acquired over those years, nothing compares to the miracle and innocence of new life.

I suppose to him, little Atlas Theodore Morris, and the rest of you reading the words I pen, the first grandmother wisdom I hope you will grasp is the value of your birthright and the power of the intentions you create in your world. We enter this space in time with a mission to live, learn, heal, and teach. The amount in which we do that is completely our choice. All of creation, angels, guides and ancestors are on this journey with us to empower, guide and direct us on that mission. All we must do is seek that guidance.

I believe that the true value of the wisdom keeper is not to keep the wisdom but to share this universal wisdom with all in the hope that it inspires others to see their value. Inspiring others with our wisdom is our great gift to the Universe.

If I could write to my younger self, or my little grandson, of all the wisdom I have gained in my years, not only would it

CHAPTER 13 | STEPPING INTO THE CRONE WISDOM

be a miracle that I remembered it all, the miracle would also be in me seeing it as wisdom.

That being said, one of the most valuable truths I would like to pass on to you would be that *all you seek is within you*. We spend so much of our life seeking wisdom, happiness, fulfillment, joy, contentment and a variety of other things through sources outside of ourselves without understanding that what we are searching for is already within us, and we just need to learn to tap into that bountiful resource.

You might be thinking, "That sounds great, but how do I tap in?"

We can tap into that inner wisdom through many pathways such as prayer, meditation, yoga, music, and nature, just to name a few. To the degree you seek your soul wisdom, you will find it.

Modalities such as prayer, meditation, crystals, tarot, yoga, Reiki, music, and chanting are just a few of the tools to help us reach that inner world.

Being aligned with your soul is a superpower. Love is a superpower! As you love yourself, you will love others. I do believe, if you don't love yourself, it will be difficult to truly love others as you will be bound by the restraint of not fully understanding or feeling the love.

Your inner world is much more important than your outer world. Just as there are many wonders to explore in our outer world, there are even more in this magical inner world. Be aligned with your soul and courageous enough to explore both worlds before you.

I believe that true wisdom comes from trusting in spirit. That connection with your source, whether *it* be called God, soul, source, spirit, creator, higher power, Mother Nature or whatever is divine to you. That intuition we feel. That inner *gut feeling* when you just know! We all have it; we are all born with it. Some have closed it off through conditioning, while others embrace it and allow it to be their guide. I believe that from back before conception, we are spiritual beings. A spiritual being, think about that for a moment! You are a spiritual being created for the purpose of living this life. You came to this life to live, learn, heal and teach, and your creator, angels, guides, and ancestors are all with you to empower you to do that. How powerful is that! How truly amazing is that! You are a spiritual being living life as a human and not the other way around. You are not a human trying to find the spiritual, but a spiritual soul living this human experience. It's all kind of *mind-blowing* when you think about it. Yet it's also very empowering knowing that you are not alone in this journey of life.

Mindfulness has been one of my greatest teachers. Learning the practice of mindfulness allows for the great wisdom we seek to come from our soul. Learning to *pause, connect, and be mindful* has been another one of the greatest bits of wisdom I have gathered in my life, I just wish I had found it before I was in my fifties, yet as with many lessons in life, it came when it was supposed to. Learning to pause and connect with my inner soul in every situation in life has helped me to see things as they really are and not just as I think or hope they are. Mindfulness helps me to get out of my head as I remember that my

CHAPTER 13 | STEPPING INTO THE CRONE WISDOM

thoughts are neither right nor wrong—they just are! Often we think that our thoughts are reality, and at times, we even make them into our reality.

Being mindful of the moment allows me to release the guilt of the past and not take on the worry of the future. The practice of mindfulness is just that, something that I need to practice every day of life. The more you practice, the better you get at it; the better you get at the practice, the more it becomes a way of life. I encourage you to begin the practice of mindfulness today; it will change your life. I highly recommend the book, *Mindful Insights*, by John Shearer, as it will take you on a "52-Week Journey to Master Your Mind." This book gives you every tool you need to work through the practice of mindfulness.

In my years volunteering at hospice and working in my practice as an end-of-life doula, I have found that the greatest wisdom we gain from the dying is *how to live!*

In North America, I believe we tend to hide death away, not talk about it as if by doing so, we will escape it. Let me debunk that myth right now. Nobody, absolutely no one in this life, will escape death! We are all born, and we all will die! Once all of those superficial things that we think are so important become stripped away by the process of death, what's left is *love*, and we find that love is all that truly matters. If we live our lives truly loving ourselves and loving others, we will find that we have found both the key to happiness and the key to success. Learning how to love yourself is truly one of the greatest gifts you will ever give yourself or give others.

Another important nugget of wisdom I have gained over the years is *don't compare yourself to others.* You are not anyone else, so don't even try to be. Be authentically you! It's who you were created to be. This world doesn't need any more copycat humans; it needs authentic people living the life that they were created to live. Stop trying to fit into a box you don't belong in. Let your soul dance to the music within you. We can all be wonderfully different!

I also learned some time ago that one drop of water in the ocean *is* the ocean! Something to think about, isn't it? One would think that one drop of water in the ocean would be insignificant, yet when you think that one drop is the ocean, things radically change. If that one drop is the ocean, the ocean would be very different without it. The same can be said for you, my friend! You are not just one person in the world; you are the world! Everything you do impacts the world just as that one drop of water impacts the whole ocean. Never think that what you do doesn't matter, because it does. Never think that you don't matter because you do. Never think that you can't change your world because you can. The power of one is great! Think for a moment of all the ways that one thing, one choice, one decision, one word or one act of kindness can change a life. You, yes, you, have the power to change your world! As you change yourself, you will change and impact your world. All it takes is the power of one—one choice, one decision, one change. You can be all that you aspire to be, and you can inspire others to be all that they can be as well. As you seek wisdom, wisdom will come to you, and wisdom then flows through you. Just as all those drops of water in the ocean are the ocean, you are the world. You

CHAPTER 13 | STEPPING INTO THE CRONE WISDOM

matter—you truly do! You are worthy of feeling as important as that one drop of water. We all create a life ripple, and I encourage you to believe in your ripple effect.

I have learned that change can be difficult, yet change is inevitable. In life, we often find ourselves in situations that may seem impossible to change, but if we change our perspective on the situation, we change. Often our perspective is the only thing we can change. And that we can, if we just try! Look at situations through the eyes of another. Look at situations with curiosity and compassion. Look at situations with gratitude. Look at situations as temporary because in life, everything changes, both good and bad. Start and end each day with gratitude, and you will see your perspective change. Start each day as a clean slate unencumbered by the past and end each day thankful that you did the best you could, letting go of all that caused you to feel any inadequacy. Start and end each day with a clean slate and a pure heart of love.

Be perfectly imperfect! Let go of perfection and embrace your imperfections. There is freedom in acceptance of self. Embracing your imperfections does not mean that you drop self-improvement; it simply means that you accept yourself on the journey.

Don't give your worries too much head space. If you do, they create a *monkey mind* which will continually play you a recording of negative thoughts and worries. Most things in life never happen as bad as we anticipate they will anyway, so leave the worry. Worry steals the joy and magic of today. Live for today!

Always live in hope. Allow that spark of hope to remain lit in your soul. If you feel it dimming, start a gratitude journal, read a hopeful book, volunteer for a charity, surround yourself with hopeful people. Hope is contagious, and if you surround yourself with hopeful people, who feed your soul, they will ignite that hopeful flame within you. Every situation can change on a dime. Trust in that!

Love yourself! Love yourself enough to create an environment of self-love. Learn to nourish your soul love. Remember that you can't pour from an empty cup; you can't serve others if you forget to nourish yourself. A friend once told me to let my cup overflow to the saucer and feed others with that overflow; that way, your own cup never runs dry. I love that mind-picture of people coming to drink of life and gain support and comfort from my saucer.

Let go of judgments. Unless you walk in the shoes of another, you can't truly know their circumstances. Meet judgment with the understanding that you may not know the whole story. Allow love, understanding and compassion to take the place of judgment.

Live life with curiosity and a sense of adventure. Awaken every day with gratitude for a new day and embrace the adventure of it, full of curiosity for this wonderful life you have to experience. Be curious about things you don't understand. It's been said that "curiosity killed the cat," but I challenge that line, or we would see a lot of dead cats lying around. I believe that curiosity can kill fear. I believe that curiosity can kill judgment. If we learn to embrace life with curiosity, we fear less.

CHAPTER 13 | STEPPING INTO THE CRONE WISDOM

I awoke this morning hearing someone singing the song, *What a Wonderful World*. As you read the lyrics of that song, let the meaning sink deep into your soul:

"I see trees of green

Red roses too

I see them bloom

For me and you

And I think to myself

What a wonderful world

I see skies of blue

And clouds of white

The bright blessed day

The dark sacred night

And I think to myself

What a wonderful world

The colors of the rainbow

So pretty in the sky

And also, on the faces

Of people going by

I see friends shaking hands

WISDOM KEEPERS

Saying *how do you do*

They're really saying

I love you

I hear babies cry

I watch them grow

They'll learn much more

Then I'll never know

And I think to myself

What a wonderful world

Yes, I think to myself

What a wonderful world.

(*What a Wonderful World*, words and music by Bob Thiele and George David Weiss.)

There is wisdom in looking at the wonder of the seemingly little things in this world. If we think for a moment about those little things, we can truly appreciate how truly wonderful this world is. I encourage you to seek all the wonders in this wonderful magical world we get to experience. I encourage you to see the little things for the great things that they are.

In this life, we will and do face many obstacles; the key is learning to see those obstacles as Blessings. Know that

CHAPTER 13 | STEPPING INTO THE CRONE WISDOM

obstacles can be Miracles that come to us in the form of trials. When we are able to change the way that we look at those obstacles, we see them differently, and we learn from them. I would like to remind you that all things in life happen *for* us, not *to* us.

If I could speak with my younger self, I would tell her to worry less about the future and live more in this present wonderful world! That, my friend, is the wisdom I share with you.

And last but not by any means least, I share some nuggets of wisdom from others that I love.

"If you listen carefully, the silence can be beautiful."

"Everything will be okay in the end; if it's not okay, it's not the end."

"Sometimes people can't love you the way you need them to; they love the way they can."

"Silence can speak louder than words."

"Let love be your guide, and you won't get lost."

"Awareness is the first step to action."

"Feelings are neither right nor wrong; they just are."

"The quieter you become, the more you hear."

"Be light in the darkness"

"If you change the way you look at things, the things you look at change."

"What you seek is seeking you."

"Do the best you can until you know better; when you know better, do better."

"Decide what kind of life you want, and say no to everything that isn't it."

"Live life with courageous intention."

"Courage is what it takes to stand up and speak; courage is also what it takes to sit down and listen."

"Life is not measured by the number of breaths we take, but by the moments that take our breath away."

"Sometimes, you will never know the value of a moment until it becomes a memory."

"A satisfied life is better than a successful life. Because our success is measured by others, but our satisfaction is measured by our own soul, mind and heart."

"Believe in yourself, and you will be unstoppable."

"A wise person knows that there is something to be learned by everyone."

"If you want to fly, you have to let go of what weighs you down."

"Wear gratitude like a cloak, and it will feed every corner of your life."

Chapter Fourteen

Ancora Imparo –
Yet, I Am Learning
By Melissa Nelson Curran

Melissa Nelson Curran

This essay is a reflection of a lengthy journal Melissa wrote while documenting her first teaching experience out of college. Names have been omitted or changed. Today, she has over sixteen years in the classroom.

In addition to urban teaching, Melissa also spent time in urban-suburban; and most recently, in a suburban community. She has been a Response to Intervention consultant as well.

Initially, she was hesitant to publish because she really doesn't consider herself to be a keeper of wisdom. Just a person reflecting on a life experience.

In her words: I will forever remember my first suburban teaching interview, at the time coming directly from urban. I was shunned by one of the interviewers who retorted, "We don't have problems like [yours] here."

No matter the educational setting, the core issues do not vary much. Kids still desire the same: to feel accepted and understood despite their struggles.

Ancora Imparo – Yet, I Am Learning
By Melissa Nelson Curran

Dedication:

"High school is gonna tear you up" —Ms. G

A picture of my classroom consisted of a population of African American students (approximately ten to fifteen per class) who had abilities across the board — the brushstrokes were varied. For example, I had a fifteen-year-old in sixth grade and an eighteen-year-old in eighth, as well as exceptionally talented kids. One thing they all had in common: a plethora of previous negative experiences.

I learned Milwaukee was the third most segregated city in the nation and the seventh poorest (relating to cities comparable in size). It was a challenge I never imagined being fully immersed in during my first teaching position, especially as I had no urban training or experience in my life. In fact, I had a slight, midwestern Yooper accent.

I worked for a learning academy with special students I cherish, who needed extra special care and attention, within a social services agency. I walked through a metal detector every day, passed by the food pantry, and downstairs to a narrow hall and small section of the newly renovated building. The community respected this facility and wanted to keep it. It was desperately needed here. Each student had

CHAPTER 14 | ANCORA IMPARO – YET, I AM LEARNING

his or her bag thoroughly checked before entering. (One of our students was arrested within six blocks with a gun after school hours.) But not one student ever brought something like this inside.

Students laughed at and mimicked my accent (and I laughed with them). This took them aback, not realizing at the time that I was being completely non-reactionary, which was the opposite of their anticipations. They wanted me to react, to reaffirm their preconceived notion of another white person, or even an adult, who was untrustworthy. I understood my approach was going to be vital to gain their acceptance. And if they did not trust me, there was no way they would want to learn.

I studied my pages of notes with specific teacher feedback regarding each child.

And in the spirit yet of learning, I discovered what a doo-rag is. This was after I mistook one for an arm sling since I saw it tied around a student's neck! My unassuming nature could either have helped or hurt me, but I decided to remain open and curious. Quite a few of my students had lost a sibling to gun violence, and many made shirts memorializing their loved ones. It was a tragic, harsh reality. This was life every day; there was no break.

I overheard a young sixth grader discussing a stabbing murder he saw at a bus stop corner in his neighborhood. And there was another innocent student — whose name means "wise one" in Arabic (he was very proud of this) — who found a gun by the Milwaukee River and turned it in to police. He was still awaiting his reward. "They promised," he faintly whispered. I couldn't help but ache for his disappointment. This was a kid who needed to see credible, congruent adults who cared and followed through with their actions.

I learned AAVE (African American Vernacular English) from my last class, such as "Where do you rep?" This means, "Where do you live?" "Juken" means "cool" or "a lot of fun." "You've got hands" means "You're tough." If someone is being "silly" or "crazy," you bob your head and say, "You's a goon." I didn't say it quite right, though, or with proper head movements, so they said I should watch *Beauty Shop*. Whitney laughed, "I love ya, Miss Nelson." They told me once that I am the best teacher. Because not only do they learn from me, but I learn from them.

A month in, kids had started calling me "perma-smile." They thought I laughed a lot. One girl said she thought I smiled all the time because I was trying to conceal my sadness. It made me wonder if that's why *she* smiled, and if hidden behind her wide-eyed grin I saw every morning was a soft and vulnerable little girl.

Chunking directions, modeling with graphic organizers, differentiating, checking for understanding, having well-established routines, remaining calm yet steadfastly firm and approachable, and trusting kids with tasks like being the geography bingo caller if he or she won, had been successful. Eventually, I received a SMART board, and kids loved it when we took virtual field trips using Google Earth. I asked them where in the world they wanted to zoom in on this gargantuan blue sphere, like we were in a simulation together, flying high above our planet. It was better than the IMAX; my kids were autonomous.

CHAPTER 14 | ANCORA IMPARO – YET, I AM LEARNING

They were acutely in tune with people and could easily sniff out someone who was "phony," too rigid, fears them, or doesn't care, and they were unabashedly honest about it. Passive-aggressive was not in their speech.

Kids had been giving a new colleague who taught geometry at the end of the hall an *extremely* hard time. She was the farthest from our administrator's office, and I felt for her. We were talking about how difficult it could be to teach the kids because many had unimaginable backgrounds and experiences. For instance, Samantha, strikingly beautiful, saw her older sister get shot and killed in her home by an ex-boyfriend.

These kids *needed* to feel cared about. This made me thankful I felt comfortable in the classroom; and, even more importantly, that I genuinely enjoyed my students. Another teacher popped in and reaffirmed she heard "nothing" about me — which essentially meant I was accepted. (I was also aware some will never like me; *Ancora Imparo*.)

One of my very challenging eighth-graders approached one day, "Miss Nelson, you're a really good teacher." I started laughing, unsure if he was just playing with me or was serious.

"No, really," he said, "you're a good teacher." It meant a lot to have earned his trust. Then Devon chimed in, "Yeah, except you rib too much." A little inside joke since we liked to poke fun. I knew we had a good rapport. We could also be serious. I taught him how to play chess, and he was very competitive.

Another student who said I was her favorite arrived to class, "Miss Nelson, don't move. I want to pass these papers out for you. I want you to rest." At times they made me melt!

Realizing how much they depended upon and looked up to teachers (even though most kids would not admit this), I worried about them often. I wanted to be the best mentor I could for them, always thinking of ways to positively motivate behavior and increase engagement. Some didn't understand this and would defensively push back. But I felt it was a way of testing me, especially if they were not used to this kind of attention. I try my best to remain consistent. So I showered them with kindness, anyway.

One day I asked kids, "If you could have just one wish, what would you wish for?" Instead of things one would think a middle school student may say, like "a sports car," or "to win the lottery," I received answers like, "to see a day without crime, murder, and violence," or to "visit heaven and see what it looks like," "to live with my parents," or "to have a new life and start all over." Their deep thoughts expressed how much some had already experienced at such young ages. They didn't take life for granted. I greatly admired that about them. It took courage to remain sincere.

When I had them send cards to the teacher I was hired to replace, to congratulate her for having her baby, they shared the most sentimental poems. Many were spiritual, saying things like, "Did your eyes light up when you saw her?"…an angel sent to Earth just for you," and "God has

CHAPTER 14 | ANCORA IMPARO – YET, I AM LEARNING

blessed you with the most beautiful and precious gift that will love you forever."

Parent-Teacher Conferences

Have you ever felt your mind and body were separate? That somehow your psychological being hovered above the physical, dogmatically watching the "real" you?

Parent-teacher conferences. This was how the day ended, but there are no words for where it went from there. Originally, I would have been thinking about the three-day weekend ahead. Great America was on my mind. But I had no idea what was about to happen.

I did readers theater, and I read *A Tell-Tale Heart* by Edgar Allen Poe with the seventh- and eighth-graders and a more simplistic play with the sixth graders. The day seemed to go smoothly. At three o'clock, when school finished, I stopped in the copy room to talk with Ms. D before heading up to the cafeteria for the six-hour session of parent-teacher conferences.

Ms. D asked if I was nervous, and I replied, "Not really." She smiled, squeezing my shoulder, and told me how great of a job I was doing.

"Really?" I asked.

Ms. D responded, "Of course. Everyone here, they all think you look like this is your third year teaching already! You're a natural. No one can believe this is your first." I didn't know what to say.

I met about forty different parents of students. I was surprised at how respectful they all were! They were mainly concerned with behavior issues and wanted to make sure their child was doing their work and coming to class. Many of my students who were failing were not coming to school. None of the parents questioned anything I said.

Many of the mothers seemed to have quite a few children, and I was amazed at how most worked two jobs and were still able to care for them (unless the kids were separated). There was one mother who asked why I was in Milwaukee, explaining I should have stayed "up north." When I asked why, she replied, "Because it's nice up there" and "Milwaukee is a dump."

At nine p.m., we were tired and ready to go home. Unfortunately, the neighborhood we were in was not always safest at night. Our well-respected principal took a look outside and noted there was a gang fight directly in front of one of the exits. She recommended we all wait for one another and walk out in a group.

We huddled out together from a main exit in the front. As I looked around the corner of the building, I saw a group of what appeared to be twenty kids in a large mass. I couldn't tell if there was fighting from the outside of it, but I heard a cacophony of yelling. A colleague explained that inside the crowd, kids were likely physically at each other. I hurried across the street. At that moment, I was thankful I was lucky enough to have a nice car to drive home in, and I felt safe.

The feeling didn't last long. Immediately when I got in the car, I had several messages on my cell phone. I checked the

CHAPTER 14 | ANCORA IMPARO – YET, I AM LEARNING

first one, which was from my aunt. I started getting nervous. The next message was from my cousin. By this point, my heart was pounding. She said she was waiting for me at my apartment and I needed to come home as soon as possible. My hands started shaking; instinctively, I knew something was seriously wrong. I had one person on my mind.

I called my aunt, but she said my parents weren't with her, to try them at my grandpa's. My body must have been trembling when I asked Dad what was going on.

He kept telling me to pull over. I knew he was concerned because I had an hour's drive home from work. I asked if it would be better if I talked with my cousin when I got home. He gave the answer that I didn't want, which was "yes."

My mind was on a Tilt-A-Whirl race. I felt like the faster my heart beat, the faster I wanted to drive home. But I kept control of myself, so I made it back safely. *Maybe he's just in the hospital*, I hoped.

It was aggravating driving back in traffic and getting stopped at so many scarlet lights. Each vermilion flash seemed to be mocking and snickering; *You will never make it*. At last, I arrived at my apartment.

As I got out of the car, my body floated up the jagged steps to the front door. It didn't feel like it was me. It was like I was suspended above, watching myself go through the physical motions.

I don't remember walking inside, but when I sat down on the couch, instantly I turned and blurted out, "It's my brother, isn't it? He's dead."

My cousin nodded yes. I will remember that moment for as long as I live. I screamed and began crying simultaneously; I had never felt so many intense emotions. A poignant pain plunged into my chest, reaching deep into the pit of my stomach, where it settled like an acidic lemon. I felt like something had been carelessly cleaved from me. Suddenly, I had to stand up because my stomach started to do flips, tighten, and shift — I was about to vomit.

I torpedoed into the bathroom, where I hung my head over the toilet. Wrapping my arms around the solid, cold porcelain seemed to be all that was reassuring I was okay. My cousin reached for me and said she didn't care if I threw up on her, so I let my head rest in her lap and released myself of all my frustration, anger, and grief.

Then came all the questions: Why didn't I get to say goodbye? Did he know how much I loved him? Was he okay? *He was just twenty.*

I didn't mean to sound angry when speaking with my father, but he said that by the tone of my voice, he almost thought I wasn't coming back home. After the tears, I became indignant! What about the mess and pain my family would have to deal with for the rest of our lives? The hole that will eternally ache…weddings, graduations, careers, so much ahead. Life felt like it was abruptly upchucked. A divisive line obliterated it into two halves: before and after.

CHAPTER 14 | ANCORA IMPARO – YET, I AM LEARNING

I didn't make it to my grandpa's until well after two in the morning. As I set my things down by the sofa, Mom and Dad both came into the living room. They looked sullen and exhausted. Their faces seemed to have aged ten years since I had last seen them two weeks earlier. *Just a couple of weeks ago, when we were still a whole family.* I can't explain the hurt and sadness I felt seeing them that way. For the first time in my entire life, I saw Dad cry. They walked up to me with arms outstretched, crying so severely their shoulders were austerely trembling. I grabbed them both, and we hugged for a long time.

Coming full circle, I empathized with my students even more. I couldn't wait to get back to them. After a lot of crying for several days, making funeral arrangements, having to go through my brother's things — that was the hardest — loss of sleep, loss of appetite, I was ready to go back.

I missed three days of work, almost a week of respite with the long weekend. My students got me through this time. I kept thinking, *Things are hard, but I don't have to worry about drive-bys. I'm not a minority living in the projects.* They gave me energy and purpose.

Most were exceptionally quiet when I returned, and I was surprised at Josh and Calvin, who came in after school to spend extra time in my room. "Are you gonna be around for a while, Ms. Nelson?" they asked. "Is it all right if we hang out for a little while and play checkers?"

I replied, "Sure," after I first took advantage of this sudden dedication and made them catch up on some work. I couldn't help but wonder if this was their way of showing they cared.

Some were vocal. "You left us! I was so depressed! I didn't want to come to school."

Initially, I did not know how to approach the situation with my kids. But I am glad I told them the truth. I wanted them to see white people have problems, too. And I wanted to show them how I handled it. They needed me, and I needed them. They taught me how important it is to separate yourself from what is going on around you and accept things you cannot change. And even more crucial, they taught me the importance of being able to connect with others who have experiences different from ours.

I will be forever appreciative to the students and staff who taught me so much, especially during a time I was fresh in a city and a building where initially I felt like an anthropologist. The deepest gratitude for being patient with me and for the wind beneath my wings.

Chapter Fifteen

Our Childhood Memories and Their Wisdom: My Kindergarten Tour
By Pedram Owtad

Pedram Owtad

Pedram has been happily married for over 16 years with two precious sons, nine and two years old, and is dedicated to family, personal growth, and giving back to society.

Always fascinated with human behaviors and spirituality, and paradoxically as a computer engineer drawn into technology and innovations, Pedram has always believed in human goodness at the core and that there is good in everything. He spoke about his life experience on this subject matter at a DebX talk called, *Life is Happening For Us, Not To Us*.

Pedram has always been passionately interested in meditation and searching for the answers in the silence within. He started sharing his experiences by leading visualization meditations during monthly events of a friendly gathering called, *Together, Just Be*, which led to a calling to bring meditation to a broader audience through social media called, *Unity Meditation*.

Pedram is driven by famous questions such as: "Who am I? What's my purpose in life? How can I make a difference? How do we unleash the magical powers we're all innately been given as human? What am I here to learn? And, how can I serve?"

With these constant questions in mind, there have been fascinating answers, especially within the past eight years, with most of them being rooted in his childhood memories. One of them is shared within this book, which Pedram believe points to our child self who, in states of innocence, curiosity, joy, and love, silently records the wisdom we need in this physical life experience, and most effectively, forms our future toward what we need to experience and learn from.

Pedram is deeply honored to share this childhood memory and its lifelong effect on his life. His intention is to point out that, even in the simplest and joyous memories, is hidden wisdom that will reveal itself once we're ready.

Stay divine,
Namaste
Pedram Owtad
UnityMeditation.com

Our Childhood Memories and Their Wisdom: My Kindergarten Tour
By Pedram Owtad

"I'm walking through a kindergarten with my mother, in the company of a school teacher who is giving us a tour of the school. The teacher and my mother are talking in the background, and I'm excited and fascinated, observing this new place, with colorful walls and all kind of drawings and artwork on the walls.

I would like to run and bounce from room to room, inside and out, but I must stay close to my mom; it's a new and strange place, after all.

They let me walk into a class, and I see other kids about my age, three to four years old, all happy, excited, confused, gazing at me, wondering who I am, wondering where they are, where their parents are, and what are they supposed to be doing, sitting around a table which seemed like a big table and its height was to the waist of one of the kids that were standing next to the table. On the table were a lot of colored pencils and white papers. Some of the papers had all kinds of fascinating drawings on them—none of them looked like an actual shape to me, but they were colorful.

It seems this is supposed to be my class, and these kids are my friends. I'm excited beyond words and want to go and sit with the kids and join their drawing fun.

CHAPTER 15 | OUR CHILDHOOD MEMORIES AND THEIR WISDOM

But I must follow my mom, who was still following the teacher.

I'm so excited to get to know my new friends that I didn't even pay attention to the rest of the school while we were walking through it until we walked out of the building; wow, so colorful, so green, I'm happy, excited, let go of my Mom's hand and run to play in this colorful playground, running around, switching from swing to slide, from slide to the red, yellow and brown wooden horse that wobbles when I sit on it. There are so many new things to play with that I can't make my mind which one to choose first.

In the corner of the playground, my mother is still talking to the teacher, but I'm so excited about everything that I don't care what they're talking about—you know, adult stuff."

And the memory fades while I'm still playing

That's one of the first vivid childhood memories that I can recall with details, very happy and colorful, but I'm not sure why I never went to that kindergarten, and as a matter of fact to no other kindergarten, until I went to preschool for a short time, and then the first grade, and it took me 40 years to understand why I didn't go to that kindergarten and why I couldn't remember anything else from that specific day.

Our fascinating mind instinctively has only one purpose, and that's to keep us safe—from events, from predators, from dangers, and even from ourselves and our memories and emotions attached to those memories. It either triggers fight or flight mode or turns into a professional editor that will hide and censor whatever memory that might hurt us, or if our analytic mind may judge, that it will not serve us.

I was born and raised in Tehran, Iran, but at the time, we were in Pakistan due to my dad's Ph.D. degree and job, and even though we had a great lifestyle, my mom and my dad were going through some relationship challenges, and at times, the home energy wasn't all-loving and colorful, and as a result, I have a lot of blind spots in my childhood memories.

But the ones that I do remember contain life-changing messages and childhood programs that have altered the course of my life. For some of them, I found their secret message, and some of them are still a mystery.

"The mystery of life isn't a problem to solve, but a reality to experience." ~ Frank Herbert, *Dune*

And experience it, we all do, that's what life is all about, and it's up to us to decode what's there to be learned from that experience and how to elevate our spiritual beingness.

Throughout my educational years, all the way from first grade to the graduate years, I liked school. I studied hard, I was a good student, and I always studied five times more than most other students, but my grades were always average, way below the effort I put into it. And my question was, why? I could never figure out the hidden dark force that was holding me back by enforcing a lack of confidence and a sense of "I am not good enough."

I used to read a passage or memorize a math formula 50 times, and I knew it by heart, but a voice in my head would

CHAPTER 15 | OUR CHILDHOOD MEMORIES AND THEIR WISDOM

misguide me otherwise. "I think you're going to screw this up on your test. You didn't repeat it enough, come on try another few more times," said the voice in my head, and as a result, I always faced a shortage of time to review my subjects or finish my tests in a timely manner—an OCD behavior, if you will, during studying or even during the tests.

From the initial big bang of an event onward, the effect keeps expanding unless we consciously intervene. In my case, my child-self's observation and understanding in that kindergarten was the big bang of this affirmation or behavioral pattern. The voice in our head tends to prove itself right every time, so it will look for events, opportunities, or even our unparented weaknesses to get us into a condition to fail and then get louder in our head repeating, "Didn't I tell you so? You're not good enough in this field."

It keeps repeating the point so that we won't even be able to see the origination of this big bang anymore, or even worst, we actually believe it's the truth.

So, about 40 years passed and during this time, even though I graduated and had many successes, I always struggled with this spell coming out from the dark and hidden closets of my memories almost every time I had an exam or had to speak in front of the class or a group of audience. Studying until the last minutes before the exam, running out of time during exams, and trembling, stuttering and even shaking during any talk or presentation in front of more than five people.

Even though it was hurting every time, I blamed it on my poor memory—that I should have studied more, that I should work on my confidence, that my past is affecting this, maybe I'm not sleeping enough, maybe because my father didn't encourage me to speak in front of an audience and many other reasons that were just trying to hide the source and affirm my failure.

Then I attended a three-day seminar, with over 100 people to dig into our deepest personal questions so that we may find the answer and alter our life or gain peace of mind.

The seminar leader explained how we live in the past by bringing our past to our future, how our parents and our environment could have affected our life path and habitual patterns, and about the chattering of the voice in our head. Attendees shared their memories, questions, and A-ha moments, and the seminar leader would professionally ask certain questions to help us dig under the hidden layers, the ones that alter our life path and make us confused, unhappy, dissatisfied and make us repeat the similar mistakes over and over again.

On my first day, the voice in my head kept repeating that I know all this, I've read it in books, and it does not apply to me.

On the second day, I think some of the attendees' sharing and seminar leader's questions started to sink in and get underneath my thickened layers of hidden memories and soften them up. Occasionally, when someone was sharing, the voice in my head went quiet, and I felt I could relate to that story. It was both exciting and scary to feel I'm discovering something new about myself, I may find that

CHAPTER 15 | OUR CHILDHOOD MEMORIES AND THEIR WISDOM

I've been wrong about certain things for about 40 years, and that now I must have a breakthrough and find a new approach to my future and my life and change some of my most rigid habits.

On the third day, I guess the voice in my head went totally silent—maybe it felt that I was ready to face some truths, and I was strong enough to have some breakthroughs. Some of my memories came up so vivid and detailed as if I was there. I could hear the unheard, and I could see the unseen. It was as if my subconscious was recording everything, to the tiniest details, and was now playing them back to me.

It felt like all the dots were connecting, and each one was an explosion of a firework in the sky and the firework I had. On the third day, I had so many fireworks and surfaced memories that I felt weak as a newborn. I stood up to share my excitement and fears with the seminar leader. I was shaking so bad that I could barely stand, and I broke into tears. Tears of joy, confusion and fear, but that was a breakthrough for me, and I found the answers to several of my lifelong personal questions.

Regarding this colorful memory of my kindergarten visit, I saw it again through different lenses. I saw my five-year-old self fearful of letting go of my mother's hand during the tour inside the school, but once we approached the end of the tour, I let go of my mother's hand to go and play in the playground. But this time the memory had more details, and I saw my mother and the principal of the school standing under the shade of a tree in the corner of the playground, and my mother explained to the principal, that we've moved from a different country due to my father's job, and English is not our native language, and we speak Farsi at home and that she was hoping that school could assist me learning English to communicate with the teachers and other students. But the principal's response was, "We're a highly-graded school, and we have certain requirements before we can accept a new student. One of them is knowing how to speak in English, of course to the level of a five-year-old, but since your son doesn't know even a single word of English, it would be hard for us to communicate with him even if he needs a cup of water. And it would be hard for him to communicate with other students, which might cause frustration or confusion for the staff or other students. Unfortunately, we can't accept him at this time unless you practice the basics with him at home before bringing him back to this school."

My mother thanked her with disappointment and grabbed my hand, and we left the school while I still wanted to stay and play.

What do you think that five-year-old boy understood from these simple few last-minute conversations? That "I'm not good enough, I don't belong, I'm not smart enough. Those other kids know better and are better than me."

These messages sank in and hid the last-minute conversation to keep me safe from any hard feelings and left me with a joyful, colorful, and playful memory of a kindergarten tour, only to surface its voice whenever I was about to remember that conversation.

As a five-year-old boy, I didn't know any better, my mother never thought I would hear that conversation or

CHAPTER 15 | OUR CHILDHOOD MEMORIES AND THEIR WISDOM

mean it that way, and the principal never realized the magnitude of such a simple conversation while I was playing in the playground. So, it wasn't anyone's fault, but it altered my approach to education and my social life for so long, until I was strong enough to know it, and parent myself with, "It's okay. You're okay. You're smart. You're enough." This lead me to my breakthrough, and how I approached learning after that—even speaking on the DebX stage in front of 500 people about how life unfolds for us and not to us, and even leading group guided meditations. None of that would have happened if I wouldn't have quieted the voice in my head, fearlessly surrender to the consequences, and surface and remember the source of those voices.

Everyone's life is a story to tell and a life's lesson to be learned, some with harsh and extremely tough memories that we might not even want to go there and surface them again, ever, and some that are beautiful and colorful. The reason I brought up this memory and message in this writing is to emphasize that our childhood memories, even the happy ones, have something to say, and we should listen to them. Most that I've read and heard are extremely dark and harsh ones, which, in some cases, we might even understand the depth and true pain of the writer, so I intentionally brought up this example to bring us the awareness to our childhood importance. As our own parent, we dig further, even in our memory's joyful toy boxes, to either clean them and toss them away or bring them out and treasure them.

I should clarify that not all the experiences or voices in our heads are negative. In the same pattern, positive events and affirmations can create big bangs of positive expansions in life as well, some aligned with our blueprint potentials and purposes in life, and some might be drifting us away from that calling.

A positive memory aligned with our blueprint calling will lead us to salvation, to a life of fulfillment, joy, and satisfaction, but a positive affirmation that's not aligned with our divine calling will make us expert, experienced and professional on that subject matter—a physical life achievement, if you will. But deep inside we always have a sense of lack and dissatisfaction, and even in the peaks of success and achievement we might feel something is missing.

So never ignore childhood memories that might surface years later—if it's surfacing, it has something to say. Dedicate a few minutes in silence and listen to it, meditate on it, remember as much as you can, take yourself back to that time and space with as much as detail as you can, but then look at it as an adult who is willing to listen to and care for that child.

And last, but not least, never forget the possible effect of your words on children around you, even if it seems they're not listening.

As Dr. Joe Dispenza says, *"Memory without emotional charges is wisdom,"* and once we reach out to our memories, detached from our emotions, we would be the ultimate wisdom keeper of that memory and all that it entails, so that we can learn from it and share it with all those who might benefit from it on their spiritual journey.

Chapter Sixteen

Becoming Wise Through My Eyes
By Talia Renzo

Talia Renzo

At a young age, Talia Renzo was bullied tremendously in school, and her dad passed away unexpectedly all in the same year. Shortly after her dad's passing, Talia was abandoned and grew into adulthood rather quickly. As she experienced great loss, it brought her to a higher appreciation for wisdom. Talia decided not to fall the same way as everyone else did through life's greatest trials. Instead, she took all her pain and channeled it into passionate writing and pearls of wisdom. Co-author of *52 Weeks of Gratitude Journal, Life Coach, Kindness Crusader*, and *365 Days of Self-Love*.

www.taliarenzo.com

Facebook: www.facebook.com/taliarenzo

It is impossible to express my gratitude to my family for believing in me, especially to my dad, who always and still does believe in me from the heavens above.

Thank you to As You Wish Publishing for giving me a space to be myself and encouraging others to do so. A special thank you to my beloved Memaw. I sat on her porch and wrote this chapter reflecting on her wisdom and the inspiration she has been in my life.

Becoming Wise Through My Eyes
By Talia Renzo

When I felt weak,

I turned to you,

When I was drowning in my grief,

It was you who pulled me up to the surface of that ocean blue.

That beautiful ray of sunshine,

Poured hope back into my empty heart.

It was wisdom that rewrote my storyline.

Faith, love, and wisdom will always stand together; they will never fall apart.

They say everything happens for a reason,

No matter if you are the victor or the victim,

Or if it's just a change in season,

There is always something to be learned from wisdom.

Life is just a human experience,

We are all here to learn.

Somethings are left definitive or mysterious,

but there is always something to be earned.

CHAPTER 16 | BECOMING WISE THROUGH MY EYES

The next time you think you are drowning,

reach your hand out,

Hope will restore and leave your heart pounding.

Listen to your heart, and let wisdom guide you through your doubts.

This is my love letter to my restored wisdom that has saved my life over and over again. The wisdom that saved me when I thought another day wouldn't pass me by and gave me wings to fly. I am so thankful for the part of my heart that has taught me to never give up, and to keep fighting, even when I feel like I have nothing left.

When I was sixteen years old, my dad died very unexpectedly. At the time of his passing, I was a sophomore in high school, and I was bullied tremendously, even just weeks after his passing. The taunting got so bad that I had to be homeschooled. I felt like I had lost everything. I had no one or nothing to turn to. I lost my faith, I lost my hope, and I lost the one person who believed in me.

Looking back at that time of my life, I just remember feeling so insecure. My voice was taken from me at a young age when a group of girls in high school bullied me, even weeks after my dad died. I was stripped of whatever was left of my self-esteem. I felt empty inside. I felt like I had nothing left to give since everything was taken away from me.

I had to learn to rebuild the foundation of who I was. It was through my experiences in my young life that I found wisdom. I had something to look forward to again in life. I took my broken pieces and glued them back together until I rediscovered the beauty that defined me. I learned that my pain and my experiences did not define who I was. I had and still have the ultimate say in what defines me. Nobody can ever take that power away from you. I learned through wisdom what the ego was not able to see. Wisdom has been the wings that have helped me to soar over life's greatest obstacles.

When I was sixteen years old, I wrote my first book about how discovering wisdom in my life saved my life. Before I wrote my first book, I did not consider myself to be a "writer," let alone an author. I will never forget the first time I ever started writing, it was a late night, and I had so much pain, anger, grief, and sadness that demanded an outlet, so I wrote a poem. It was like lightning struck, and before I knew it, I saw my feelings on paper with my own eyes. We can't always see what we feel, but I learned very quickly that wisdom is like a mirror that can portray our feelings. The reflection cannot hurt us, no matter how cracked and broken it may appear to be. The more I took to writing, the more observant I became. I studied how those around me coped with their life's greatest struggles and how they found their outlets of healing.

My mother has always been and will always be my greatest teacher in my life. After my dad passed away, she took to drinking to cope with her pain. She shut everyone out to protect herself.

CHAPTER 16 | BECOMING WISE THROUGH MY EYES

As painful as it was to watch, and even more painful to experience, she unintentionally taught me that you can harbor your experiences and become your fears, or you can use the pain from your past to heal the broken parts of you, redefine who you want to be, and live unapologetically.

My story is meant to be shared with love, compassion, and healing. My words do come from a heavy broken heart, but if my story can help any person, young or old, who has suffered from the isolation of others, or has lost a parent, or been disowned by one, you are seen and acknowledged.

Your story matters.

Your validity is valued.

You are whole and complete with wisdom.

Wisdom taught me that my feelings mattered and that they were valid. Wisdom grabbed my hand and pulled me through the darkest points of my life when I couldn't even hold myself up, let alone get out of bed. Wisdom gave me strength on the days that I lacked faith. Wisdom fed my soul when my heart was empty. Wisdom was there when nobody else was.

Wisdom taught me that toxic patterns can be broken. I am learning at a young age that it is healthy to create boundaries—it is okay to be considerate of myself and put myself first. It is okay if I don't feel like doing something that I don't feel like doing in that moment or even at all. Who I am is whole and complete. Who I decide to be is not up to my past experiences, it's not up to my parents, and it's not up to what I am going through. It is up to me. I define who I am, and I get to make that decision every day, and the beautiful thing about that decision, is that you can be whoever you are. You can live free of judgment, criticism, pain, or passed down beliefs of being told who you should be versus who you were born to be.

The great thing about wisdom is that, at any time, it can be restored. They say that no matter how bad a situation is, there is always hope if you have faith. Faith and wisdom go hand in hand and produce more hope.

We are all born with pure wisdom. It's a matter of applying your intelligence to your life's journey. One does not have to be old to be wise. Wisdom can be challenged by your ego. When the ego interferes with hope, faith, and wisdom, your life's choices can become very shallow and artificial. The ego is not an evil entity; the ego is necessary to assemble your personality. The ego only becomes toxic when you disconnect from yourself and your values. A toxic ego feeds off of power over positivity.

To make sure you are tuned in with your wisdom over your ego, remember to focus on the positive, be honest with yourself and others, don't compare, practice gratitude, and practice forgiveness. These are just some of the many ways to align yourself with the best version of yourself that you can be.

CHAPTER 16 | BECOMING WISE THROUGH MY EYES

Wisdom never runs out,

Faith is held on through the darkest storms of rain,

And even the driest drought.

Not everything lasts forever, not even this pain.

They say faith cannot be seen,

But it can be felt.

When you rely on wisdom and everything in between,

Your sense of ego starts to melt.

Your ego helps create who you are.

It's not intended to steal from your passion.

Your ego carries you in life very far.

Farther you can ever imagine.

A toxic ego exists,

It chooses its victim based on its power.

It feeds off of negativity that cannot be resisted.

It takes from those who are not chosen to strengthen and empower.

Your ego does not define you.

Practice love and gratitude,

forgive those whose apologies have outgrew,

Reflect on your beauty from a different point of view.

Wisdom gives us hope that healing is a beautiful process, even when it is linear. Whether you are healing the mends from a past relationship, your physical body, or a loss in your life. There is always something to be gained.

When I lost my dad at a young age, I grieved his loss, but I gained strength. When I was diagnosed with mental and even physical illness, I grieved the idea of a healthy life, but I gained knowledge about wellness for my well-being. These experiences do not define me, nor do they make me who I am. They were losses, but through the lens of wisdom, I found healing and appreciation.

If you are struggling with a loss in your life, whether it be a loss of a relationship, finances, good health, or the loss of a loved one, look closely and find the gain of your loss. I do not want to minimize your loss in any way, and neither should you. Definitely acknowledge your loss, and remember that your feelings are valid in your experience.

If you evaluate your loss, what can you gain? What can you apply to your life through this difficult loss? How can you do things differently to ease the pain of your loss? Like I said, with wisdom, there is always something to be gained. What can you gain more of in your life?

Wisdom can heal loss. In less than a year after my dad died, I wrote an entire book attributing the healing of wisdom through writing. I was dedicated to writing my way through my grief. My heart will always miss my dad forever and on, but writing gave me strength when all I thought I had was weakness and pain. I would have never gone through that time of grief on my own if I hadn't written my way through it. Even on the days that I felt so weak, I found the

CHAPTER 16 | BECOMING WISE THROUGH MY EYES

energy and space for myself to write. I cried when I needed a good cry, I slept when I was tired, and I wrote when my heart was mourning.

I am currently in the midst of a physical health crisis. I struggle and suffer from chronic pain. This pain was not something I started sharing with the world until recently because it was and still is such a vulnerable part of my life's journey.

This pain has been on and off for a few years but has been consistent for over a year now. Every day I wake up in pain. I have pain in my face and jaw that radiates down to my feet. Pain so extreme and sharp that I've landed in the emergency room more times than I can remember. These sharp and intense strikes of pain hit my body and my nervous system like lightning, and I know that other people struggle with this illness that has remained nameless in my life, as well as its victims.

This pain is so intense, deep, and extreme, yet invisible to the world around me. Sometimes even invisible to the eyes of my doctors. This pain has been under-diagnosed, misdiagnosed, or yet to be diagnosed, or just simply overlooked. This pain has taken days away from me, where all I can do, is just lay in bed all day. Even though I don't know what this pain means or why it is happening, I thank God because I know that somehow it will make me stronger.

I've had some days where I am in such a bad mood because I am in so much pain, but that doesn't make me any less human. In fact, it reminds me how much more of a human being I really am.

On the days where I get frustrated easier, I find myself trying to be kinder to others. Whether I am in pain or not, I try my best to always be kind. I smile and compliment people. It wasn't until I had this chronic pain condition that I thought about the people I smile at and compliment—what if they are fighting an invisible enemy? What if they are in pain too? We all need kindness, especially now more than ever.

"Be kind always. Everyone you meet is fighting a battle you know nothing about." ~ Robin Williams

The days when I lay in bed and cry are the days when I try a little bit harder to have more faith. I want to have more faith in my healing. I want to have more faith that things will get better. I want to have more faith that I will feel better soon. The same goes for the days that I am not in as much pain. I practice affirmations to strengthen my hope for healing and my faith in wisdom:

I am strong.

I am not my pain.

I am healing.

I repeat these affirmations to myself silently or even during the panic to calm my nervous system. You don't have to use these affirmations; you can use whichever affirmations best resonate with you and your needs. If you make them a regular part of your routine, I can promise you that your darkest days won't seem so dark.

CHAPTER 16 | BECOMING WISE THROUGH MY EYES

Affirmations are a direct connection to wisdom. When we find a root source of connection to wisdom, we are becoming stronger and more in tune with the needs of our mind, body, and spirit. Affirmations are a truly healing way to connect with ourselves. When we feel so disconnected from the world around us, and even from ourselves, we disconnect from reality. Reconnect with reality through empowering yourself and being kind to yourself and others, and I promise you, you will see a change come through your life.

What do you see out of your eyes today? Do you see an opportunity for weakness or strength? When you hear what other people say about you, do you take it at face value, or do you embrace the value in how you view yourself?

Wisdom cannot only be seen in your soul and your eyes, but it can be seen when you look into the world. How you view the world is how you will grow in the world, but how you let the world view you will decide how the world grows on you.

Chapter Seventeen

The Treasure You Call by
Your Name
By Michelle Ann Ryan

Michelle Ann Ryan

Michelle Ann Ryan is a mother, grandmother, retired schoolteacher with a Master of Arts degree from CU Boulder in multicultural and social diversity education specializing in special education and English as a second language. She has traveled with several nonprofits to Central Asia, supporting people-to-people connections and self-esteem work. Michelle has thirty years of experience volunteering on the boards of three humanitarian organizations. She has facilitated women's retreats and loves being with women. Michelle enjoys working with all children and families, with a particularly warm spot for mothers and young children.

Wisdom Keepers is Michelle's third contribution to As You Wish Publishing's collaboration books. She wrote *Helping Children Grieve Through Sacred Actions and Images*, also published through As You Wish Publishing. She currently lives with her husband, a beekeeper, on a farm in Boulder County. Together they support the bees and make the most delicious creamed honey and sweetest 100% beeswax candles. Michelle spends her time being an active grandmother and listening and reporting to the Universe.

The Treasure You Call by Your Name
By Michelle Ann Ryan

The first time I heard this phrase, I thought, "What did you say?"

This moment was during a guided meditation at a Virginia Satir workshop with Peoplemaking of Colorado.

I heard the facilitator say, "The world is better because you are in it. Repeat this phrase three times in your mind's voice, placing in your name: "The world is a better place because I, (place in your name), am in it."

Tears rolled down my face. I had never heard anything so beautiful.

Could this be true? My new love and truth was in the voice speaking—the words helped receive the beauty.

I had not thought of myself a treasure, let alone that the world was a better place with me in it—what a radical idea. Thirty years later, I am reminded of how this is still radical when I posted to a new friend on social media that he was a treasure. He responded that he needed to sit with that idea. To his memory, this gentlemen, my new friend, had not been called a treasure before.

I have heard this meditation and spoken it many times over the years. I am a wisdom keeper for the Virginia Satir Lineage. She revolutionized therapy in the 1970s-80s to become the family therapy so commonplace today. My first

CHAPTER 17 | THE TREASURE YOU CALL BY YOUR NAME

experience hearing, considering, and feeling these words started with in-depth self-esteem, communication, and connection to myself and others. Every day I am on this journey, I feel the profoundness of these particular words that I had come to take for granted. On first hearing, "the treasure you call by your name," my purpose in life was being called. Accepting my treasures as God gave me the path of being in a better world; making a better world became an option and clarity. I have learned to reflect positively and love each treasure in front of me each day.

I have had the honor and privilege to love children and those who care for them in treasured hood, acceptance, and realization.

I cannot tell how fulfilling it is to hold the love of the Universe in another's eyes or your arms as they relax into, "Yes, really, it is true. You are a treasure. I know this to be true."

We are born this way because of the divine magic of two cells coming together and multiplying; you have made it to this point and are love.

The essence of love is the product of love, the expression of love. All you see, hear, taste, touch, think, and feel are opportunities of love. The Universe does not make mistakes. The Universe creates treasures. Have you explored your treasured hood? Are you ready with your magnifying glasses, detective hat, boots, and journal to begin?

I encourage you. Maybe it begins in exploring another creation from spirit and finding the sameness in you. If so, there is truth in here.

One way is to find the special place in your environment, the special place in you, and listen. Listen to your breath and heartbeat. Use your mind's eye to draw your favorite items around you. Take the time to notice the colors and textures, the smells and sounds that bring you comfort and pleasure—resting in this special place that is all you own.

I have collected an example of meditation from my experiences with Virginia Satir's work and writings, explicitly, pages 338-339 of *The New Peoplemaking*, workshops with Peoplemaking of Colorado, my yogic practices, and spiritual practices.

I give this to you to make your own.

The Treasure I Call by My Name

Prepare your environment and body for rest. You are maybe lighting a candle, spraying essential oils or rose water into the air, burning incense or sage and finding a comfortable sitting position for your body, or laying on a sheepskin or blanket and feeling the floor beneath your feet or body and the ground below the building. Or perhaps you are outside laying directly on Mother Earth. Notice the airflow on your skin and the temperature of the land. Begin to follow your breath and allow yourself to watch the breath and feel the changes in your muscles and skin as your attention is on your breath. You pay attention to tight or tender parts in your body and encourage more breath to nourish these parts to softness. Continuing to the extent, you exhale, and breathe longer—maybe up to the count of four. With this extension, more room for a longer, fuller inhale breath continues cycling your breath longer and allowing my nourishment and relaxation to your body.

CHAPTER 17 | THE TREASURE YOU CALL BY YOUR NAME

Your mind may begin to let go as your bodily tensions are relaxed. Feel yourself held by the energies, gravity, and Earth.

"Now silently go inside and give yourself a message of appreciation that might sound something like this: 'I appreciate me,' giving your spirit strength from your actions." ~ Virginia Satir

Going deeper inside your body, feel the flow of your internal space cueing to you your aliveness. Let go of breathing yourself and notice what is living you. There is more to this world. Notice the mechanics of your body that happens every day without attention or need to be in charge of doing. Begin to notice your beingness. Resting, you will soon go deeper inside your experience as you listen to the sounds, feel the sensations, and see images that move through you. Being curious and trusting that all of this energy is available and is known for healing and insight.

"As you approach this sacred place, notice your resources: your ability to see, hear, touch, taste, and smell, to feel and to think, to move and to speak and to choose."

"Linger long enough at each of these resources to remember all the many times you used them, how you are using them now, and know that they will be available to you in the future. Then let yourself remember that these resources are part of you and are capable of many new insights, sounds, and more. Realize that you can never really be helpless as long as you recognize you have these resources." ~ Virginia Satir

Now going to explore yourself more, going deeper inside your core sensations in your center, belly, and heart connection to a particular place that only you can go. You may have been here before and are very familiar with this place, or this may be a new place for you—your first time. You are looking around and seeing where you are. Knowing you are in the right space, amazed yet not surprised by the beauty of a place of your own. Take in the details of your area—the sunlight or moonlight, lamps or candles, the smells of cookies baking or dirt on the forest ground. You may be feeling pine needles perhaps or the cushions of your grandmother or grandfather's favorite chair. Maybe a bath or flowing water is nearby. What sounds do you hear? Do you hear music, birds, or is it very still and quiet, and you only hear your heartbeat and breath? Your place is filled with details of your pleasures, trusting all that comes to you at this moment is ideally perfect for you and with you. Your unique space, everything you like, is in this space. You are allowing the golden magic or your internal experience to flourish. Bathe in the mystical presence of you connected to source.

This is where you keep the treasure you call by your name. Is there a treasure box, an envelope, a door, a toolbox, a clubhouse, a book with your name on it? Go to this item and see, hear, touch, read, and take in your treasure. You are fully feeling your treasured hood. What are the details and feelings you want to remember? As you are resting here and absorbing your full treasured hood. Remember, you are a member of the collective Universe.

As you fully experience yourself as this extraordinary being, "I want you to look around for a perfectly reflective surface. It may be a pond nearby, an antique mirror next to your comfy chair, or a hand mirror in your pocket or glass.

CHAPTER 17 | THE TREASURE YOU CALL BY YOUR NAME

Looking with your mind's eye, seeing yourself precisely as you are with nothing added or taken away, with a gesture of appreciation and repeating to yourself with your internal voice, 'The world is a better place because I, (and place in your name), am in it.' Send and receive this message three times to yourself." ~ Steven Young

Having received this message, slowly bring one hand to your heart and the other to your belly. Feeling the presence of energy in your hand on your body, knowing you are a treasure. Having followed the path inside your actual being, you can now return any time you want. Your special place is to have and hold, to tend and care for, to move through life with this knowledge of your true nature. You can visit this nurturing place any time you need a reminder. You can add comforts and joys to this experience of yourself as you please. You can comfort yourself during times of stress and hardships. You can bring your successes and letdowns, being fully yourself and self-supporting.

For a few moments, pace your breath to your heartbeat, feeling the connection to life itself.

As you are ready to return your breathing to normal, slowing without haste to return to this present moment brings your experience of treasure hood into your life.

End of meditation.

My experience with conceptual meditation always brings peace, love, and amazement. We humans need validation from ourselves and each other. When we are babies and need others to survive and love us, we grow and learn to care for and love ourselves and others. The older I get, the more internally tending to my source is attractive and necessary. I experience the power I carry for myself and those I connect within the physical and energic. Age changes how we can work and tend to express creation physically. I do not cook all the meals or clean all the floors or teach all the children as I once did; however, the power of being a wisdom keeper is the gift I give. Being able to rest in patience and presence with my grandchildren without worrying about dinner or dirty laundry. I am waiting for the toddler to come for a diaper change as I tap on the changing mat on the floor instead of the chase and change. Taking the time to place a hand on the backs of children working hard on their homework. Or willingly sit by the bed of a dear elder as their breaths are labored and fewer and fewer. All these experiences are the knowledge and expression of the treasure hood of humankind connected and one with all the living and spirit world.

Through inhabiting the treasure hood, I experience more joy in living and being me. I see what life and others offer more fully with appreciation. Appreciation and gratitude for experiences that at one time were complicated and now add to my wisdom and depth of love, adding empathy and guidance which follow in my footsteps.

Another benefit of my treasure-ness is seeing myself fully and accepting when I need help and asking for it. Seeing myself with kindness and awe, it is okay to need assistance. It is enjoyable to be teachable and a beginner again. It is changing the experience from not enough to curious. How fun is that? Very fun! Then comes the laughter and joy in experiencing life. The desire to take risks on my behalf, give new activities a try, and maybe a few retries with a fresh perspective bring joy to life. As I can accept myself

CHAPTER 17 | THE TREASURE YOU CALL BY YOUR NAME

needing and wanting help, I can gently guide others to receive and get community support.

The other day, I noticed that I had been taught some hyper-responsible behaviors when I was younger and did not know better and was overly responsible for others in ways that did not serve them or me. For a moment, I cringed, and then with love, I remembered I could not change the past and recognized I was still being over-responsible. Interesting, right? So, what can I do at this moment? Awareness, acceptance, and change action. I can be myself now who wants to experience freedom and joy in myself. I can be joyful and kind now to myself and others and only be responsible for my life force. I can be a heroine of joy. That is my new name and motto from martyr to heroine of joy—that is what I choose! I can teach and model living a joyful life by making choices that bring me joy transparently. I amend my prior decisions and parenting.

I begin each day by connecting to spirit and appreciation. I ask for support from my higher guidance. I gaze at the morning sky and trees, leaves, and light out my window listening to the sounds of nature, chickens, and songbirds. I give this time to myself so that I can be the most energy-filled treasure possible. Doing this remembering and sensing each morning ensures that no matter what the day brings, I bring to it knowledge of my value and worth, and mirror that to those I touch to the best of my abilities. Am I perfect? No, but I am worthy and have value. With this knowledge, I can more freely welcome others' worth and value. I can reflect upon them. Do I do this alone? No, I have spirit helpers and loved ones and special workers all around me that I lean on and am open to receiving. On occasion, when a surprise begins my day, or a gloom encourages me to forget and pass on the light of the morning, I will be reminded throughout the day the price of skipping the critical moments in the first lights to my day to remember me and blue skies.

I share the life-earned experience of you, Dear Reader, with love.

Journal Prompts:

- After going to my treasure spot, I learned I like—
- I will nurture my treasure by—
- If I were to act as a treasure, what new choices would I make today?
- How would my life be different if I believed I was a treasure?
- Make a list of how your treasure hood is evident to you.

I appreciate Steven Young for bringing the work of Virginia Satir alive for me over 30 years of relationship and care. Satir, Virginia (1988). *The New Peoplemaking*. Mountain View, Ca. Science and Behavior Books. Inc.

www.ingramcontent.com/pod-product-compliance
Lightning Source LLC
Chambersburg PA
CBHW071312110426
42743CB00042B/1295